Dedicated to this fallen, evil human being, I love you all!

Table of Contents

CHAPTER 1   DEVELOPMENT ENVIRONMENT 1

1.1 WEB SERVER...2

1.2 CREATE WEBSITE CERTIFICATE 4

CHAPTER 2   MULTIMEDIA ELEMENTS 8

2.1 <AUDIO> ELEMENT 9

2.2 <VIDEO> ELEMENT 15

2.3 <TRACK> ELEMENT 20

CHAPTER 3   MEDIA STREAM...27

3.1 MEDIADEVICES INTERFACE 28

3.2 MEDIASTREAM INTERFACE 33

3.3 MEDIASTREAMTRACK INTERFACE 34

3.4 MEDIARECORDER INTERFACE 41

CHAPTER 4   WEB AUDIO API..50

4.1 MUSIC THEORY KNOWLEDGE 51

4.2 AUDIOCONTEXT OBJECT..56

4.3 AUDIONODE OBJECT 60

4.4 PLAY MUSIC FILES 63

4.5 CONTROL VOLUME 66

4.6 SPLIT/MERGE CHANNEL 69

4.7 AUDIO VISUALIZATION 70

4.8 FILTER..74

4.9 CONVOLUTION 78

4.10 3D SURROUND 84

4.11 DISTORTION 96

Preface

Wow, the multimedia processing capabilities provided by HTML5 are very powerful. You can use the <audio> and <video> elements to play audio and video directly on the page, which is the simplest usage; you can also use several interfaces such as MediaDevices and MediaStream to record multimedia or edit media streams, which is more advanced Usage; the most advanced function is the powerful multimedia post-processing of AudioContext and other objects, so you can achieve a page that is almost comparable to professional multimedia post-processing equipment by using HTML5, CSS3 and JavaScript, such as split/merge audio channels, audio visualization, filtering, convolution, reverberation, 3D surround and distortion, etc. This book is formed by extracting the chapters related to web media from another book I wrote, "The Whole Process of HTML5 Building a Website". If you don't know the basics of HTML5, CSS3 and JavaScript, I strongly recommend you first Make up this knowledge, and then read this book.

This book covers all the media processing knowledge of HTML5, and has a considerable depth, I suggest you calm down and read and think carefully, I believe it will benefit you a lot.

Thank the Lord, thank my family, friends and my colleagues, I love you as always.

Welcome to email me to exchange: liangming.wang@gmail.com.

Development environment

You need to use a web server in development and testing on windows operating system, because some new elements of HTML5 such as <audio>, <video>, AJAX, and offline applications must be tested through the http/https protocol.

1.1 Web Server

The easiest way to build a web server on windows is to install the "Web Server for Chrome" plug-in in the chrome browser, but it does not support the https protocol and dynamic web pages. To build a full-featured web server, you need to manually install nginx, mariadb, php or python, or simply download one-click installation packages, such as winNMP, WNMP, WAMP and XAMPP, etc. The first two packages use Nginx+MariaDB+Php, winNMP also Integrate redis database and LetsEncrypt certificate tool to realize free https; the latter two packages use Apache+MariaDB+Php, XAMPP also integrates Perl language. However, I have always been worried about why the "p" in these kits is not python, because python is not a little better than php, python ranks third (as of February 2021) on the computer programming language ranking website (https://www.tiobe.com/tiobe-index/). As the saying goes, "Python engineers who don't understand the front-end are not good product managers". The download addresses of these packages are as follows:

winNMP：https://sourceforge.net/projects/wtnmp/

WNMP：https://sourceforge.net/projects/wnmp-env/

WAMP：

https://sourceforge.net/projects/wampserver/files/WampServer%203/WampServer%203.0.0/

XAMPP：https://sourceforge.net/projects/xampp/files/XAMPP%20Windows/

This textbook uses the WAMP suite. If an error message "Cannot continue to execute code because MSVCR120.dll cannot be found..." during installation, it means that vcredist_x64.exe is not installed in the operating system (please download from https://www.microsoft.com/zh- CN/download/details.aspx?id=40784 download and install it), and then install wampserver again. It is strongly recommended not to install on the C drive (assuming you are installing in the E:\wamp64 directory). After installation, click the "Wampserver64" icon on the desktop to start it, and an icon will appear on the tray in the lower right corner of the screen.，Right-click this icon can be set for global configuration such as language, left-clicking on the icon will pop up the main menu as shown in Figure 1.1.

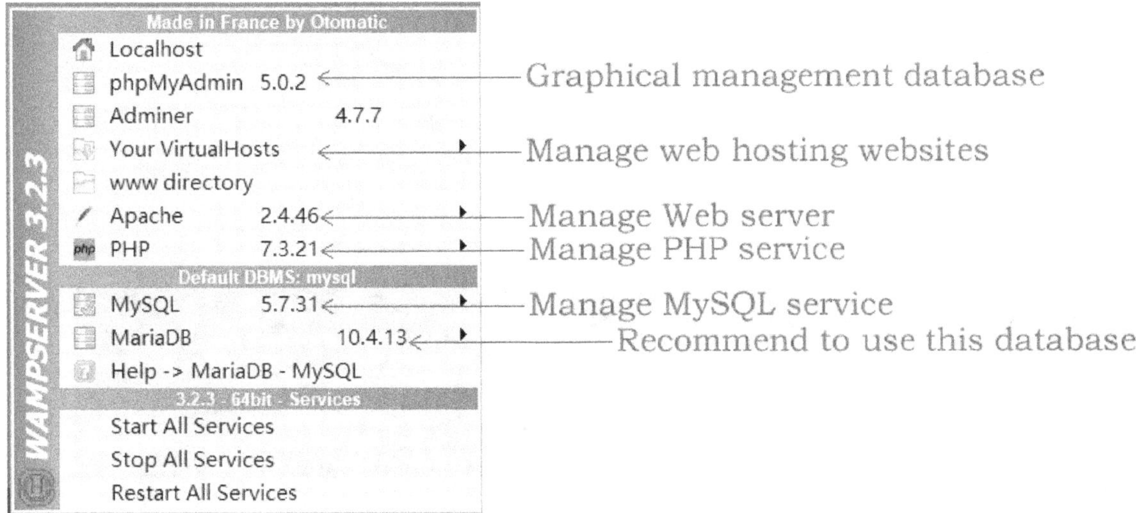

Figure 1.1 wamp main menus

Check whether the web service program is running through the method shown in Figure 1.2.

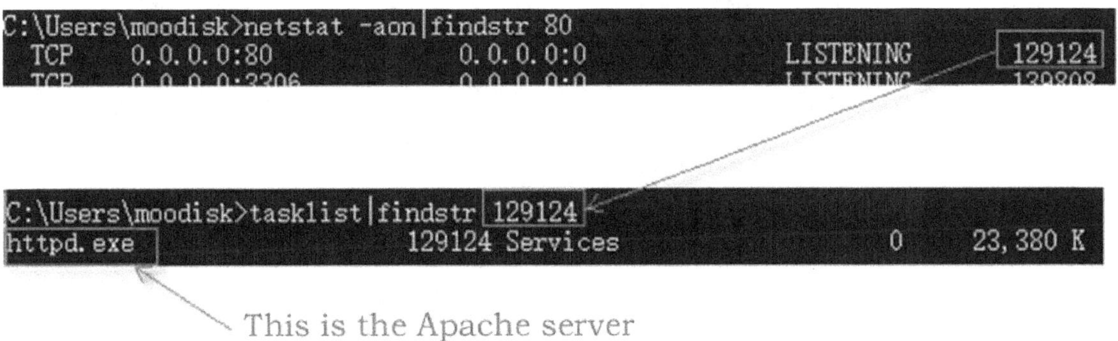

Figure 1.2 Check whether port 80 is monitored

At this time, you can open the URL http://localhost in the browser. The corresponding website directory is E:\wamp64\www, and the web files we will develop later are placed in this directory. In order to learn to test HTML5 offline applications in the future, let's add the https protocol to WampServer, so that you can access https://localhost, because many advanced HTML5 applications require the https protocol.

1.2 Create website certificate

Since the https protocol port is 443, make sure that the port 443 of your computer is not occupied. You can run the command "netstat -aon|findstr 443" to view it. For example, the situation shown in Figure 1.3 means it is occupied.

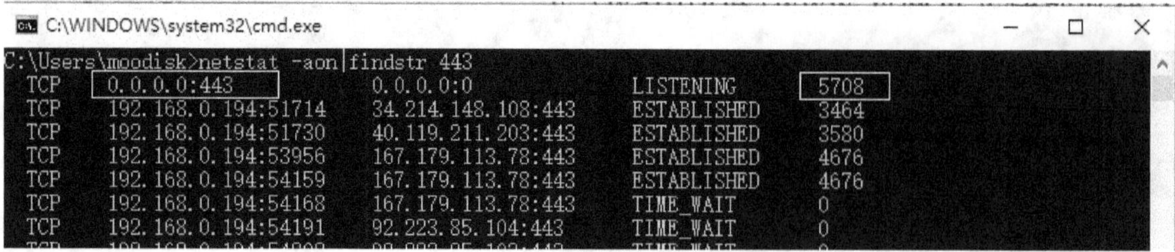

图 1.3 443 is occupied

Then use the command "tasklist|findstr 5708" to find the program name corresponding to process ID 5708:

Finally, end the process in the task manager, or uninstall the software. If the VMware Workstation is installed on your computer, port 443 will be occupied by the virtual machine software. At this time, you can modify the port 443 occupied by VMware to another number, such as 444. The specific modification method is as follows:

Start the VMware Workstation, click menu "Edit", then "Preferences", then "Share Virtual Machine", finally click the "Change Settings" button, and change 443 to 444 or other numbers. For Vmware WorkStation 16 and later, you need to modify the 443 in the file C:\ProgramData\VMware\hostd\proxy.xml to 444, and then restart the computer.

Download and install Win64OpenSSL_Light-1_1_1i.msi from the website https://slproweb.com/products/Win32OpenSSL.html, then add the path "C:\Program Files\OpenSSL-Win64\bin" to the environment variable Path, right-click "This computer", then "Properties", and then "Advanced System Settings", finally "Environment Variables" button, and then follow the operations shown in Figure 1.4.

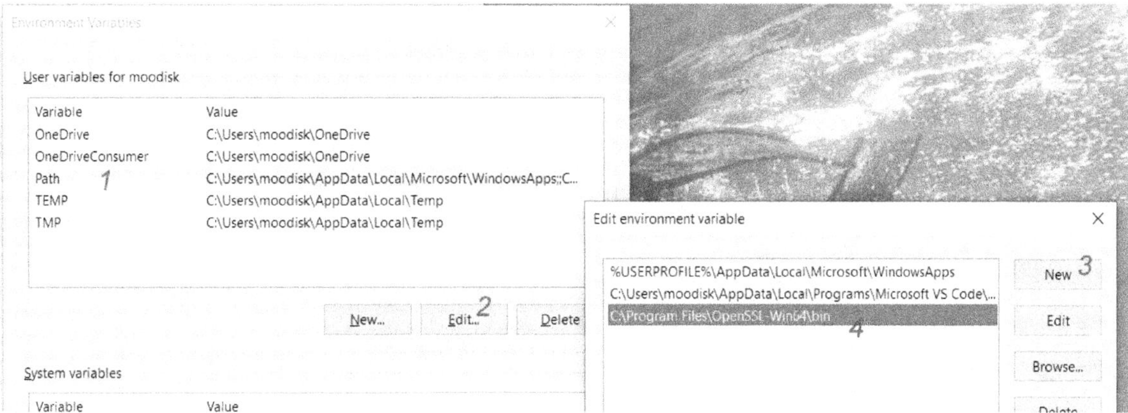

Figure 1.4 Set environment variables

Execute the cmd program to open the command window, first execute the following command to enter the E:\wamp64\bin\apache\apache2.4.46\conf directory, and then create the website certificate.

```
e:
cd \wamp64\bin\apache\apache2.4.46\conf
openssl genrsa -aes256 -out private.key 2048
```

You will be prompted to enter a protection password (Enter pass phrase for private.key:), you can enter one at will, and it is required to enter it twice.

```
openssl rsa  in private key  out server key
```

It is required to enter the password set by the previous command, and finally a one-year certificate will be issued.

```
openssl req -new -x509 -nodes -sha512 -key server.key -out server.crt -days 365
```

This command will require you to enter a serveral parameters, just press Enter, but the parameter "Common Name (e.g. server FQDN or YOUR name) []:" you must enter "localhost". In this way, we created two new files server.crt and server.key in the E:\wamp64\bin\apache\apache2.4.46\conf directory. The former is the certificate and the latter is the key.

Modify the file E:\wamp64\bin\apache\apache2.4.46\conf\httpd.conf to ensure that there is no "#" at the beginning of the following three lines.

```
LoadModule ssl_module modules/mod_ssl.so
Include conf/extra/httpd-ssl.conf
LoadModule socache_shmcb_module modules/mod_socache_shmcb.so
```

Modify the file E:/wamp64/bin/apache/apache2.4.46/conf/extra/httpd-ssl.conf to ensure that several parameters and their values are as follows:

```
DocumentRoot "E:/wamp64/www"
ServerName localhost:443
SSLCertificateFile "${SRVROOT}/conf/server.crt"
SSLCertificateKeyFile "${SRVROOT}/conf/server.key"
```

Finally restart the WampServer service. At this time, if you can open the website https://localhost, the website certificate configuration is successful, and http://localhost can also be accessed.

Extension exercise 1

To add a website accessed through the domain name www.abc.com, first create the directory E:\wamp64\www\abccom (assuming the installation directory of wamp is E:\wamp64), and place a web page file index.html in this directory , And then refer to Figure 1.5 to operate: click on the wamp icon in the bottom-right corner of the screen, then click "Your VirtualHosts", and then click "VirtualHost Management".

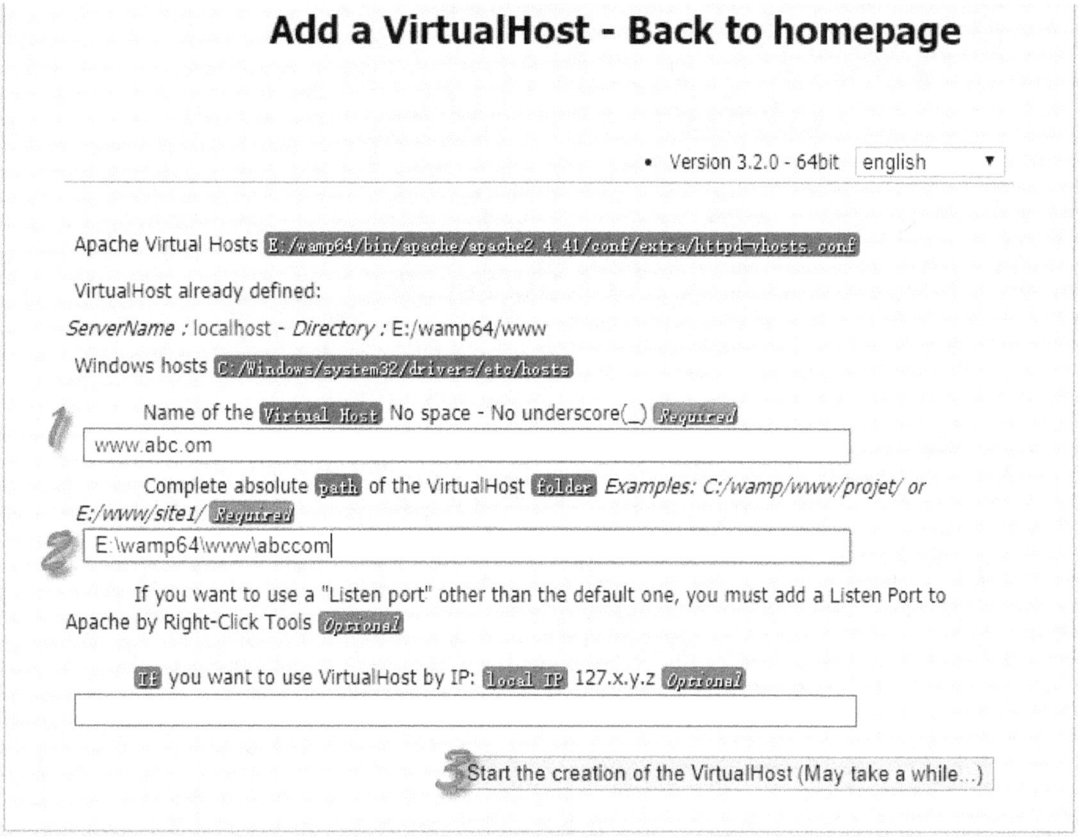

Add a VirtualHost - Back to homepage

- Version 3.2.0 - 64bit   english ▼

Apache Virtual Hosts `E:/wamp64/bin/apache/apache2.4.41/conf/extra/httpd-vhosts.conf`

VirtualHost already defined:

ServerName : localhost - *Directory* : E:/wamp64/www

Windows hosts `C:/Windows/system32/drivers/etc/hosts`

Name of the `Virtual Host` No space - No underscore(_) *Required*

www.abc.om

Complete absolute `path` of the VirtualHost `folder` Examples: C:/wamp/www/projet/ or E:/www/site1/ *Required*

E:\wamp64\www\abccom

If you want to use a "Listen port" other than the default one, you must add a Listen Port to Apache by Right-Click Tools *Optional*

`IF` you want to use VirtualHost by IP: `local IP` 127.x.y.z *Optional*

Start the creation of the VirtualHost (May take a while...)

Figure 1.5 Add a virtual website

In fact, the file E:\wamp64\bin\apache\apache2.4.41\conf\extra\httpd-vhosts.conf has been modified, and the following content has been added:

```
<VirtualHost *:80>
ServerName www.abc.om
DocumentRoot "e:/wamp64/www/abccom"
<Directory  "e:/wamp64/www/abccom/">
Options +Indexes +Includes +FollowSymLinks +MultiViews
AllowOverride All
Require local
</Directory>
</VirtualHost>
```

Next, we need to modify the file C:\Windows\System32\drivers\etc\hosts and add a line:

    10.7.57.10 www.abc.com

10.7.57.10 is the ip address of your windows network card, which should be filled in according to the actual ip of your own computer, and then restart all services of wamp (left-click the wamp icon --> restart all services). In this way, you can access your web page through www.abc.com.

Chapter 2

Multimedia elements

There are five HTML5 elements related to multimedia: <audio>, <video>, <source>, <embed> and <track>. Using these five elements, we can directly play multimedia and add subtitles on the page. This is the simplest Usage.

2.1 <audio> element

The <audio> element of HTML5 is used to play audio content in a web page. Audio resources can be specified by the src attribute of the element or defined by the <source> element. The syntax of this element is as follows:

```
<audio autoplay controls crossorigin="" loop muted preload="" src="">
   [<source src="" type="">
   <source src="" type="">
   <source src="" type="">
   ......
   Your browser does not support the audio element]
</audio>
```

If the browser does not support the <audio> element, the audio will not be played, but "Your browser does not support the audio element" is displayed on the web page (you can use elements to add styles to the prompt information, such as "<strong>Your The browser does not support the audio element</strong>") in order to remind the user. All attributes of the <audio> element and its child element <source> are optional. The attributes of the <audio> element are explained as follows:

loop - The presence of this attribute means loop playback.

controls - Display audio controls, such as play and pause buttons. If this attribute is missing, nothing is displayed on the page.

autoplay – Play automatically. However, many browsers do not support it by default now, and you need to manually turn on the browser's autoplay function.

muted – The presence of this attribute means mute.

preload - The method of loading audio can be: "none" does not load, "meta" loads audio metadata (such as file size, playback duration, etc.), and "auto" is determined by the browser to load. If this attribute is omitted, the default is "auto".

src - Specify the URL of audio resource, for example: src="Ode to Joy.mp3".

Let's take a look at the simplest example. Add code under the <body> element of the web page file:

```
<audio controls src="Piano Music-Destiny.mp3"> Your browser does not support the audio element </audio>
```

Put the "Piano Music-Destiny.mp3" file in the same directory where the web page file is located, and the effect you see in the chrome browser is shown in Figure 2.1.

Figure 2.1 <audio> element effect in Chrome

Each sub-element <source> in the <audio> element specifies an audio URL, and the type attribute of the <source> element defines the audio format. Common formats are: "audio/mp3"-mp3 audio, "audio/wav"-wav Audio, "audio/ogg"-ogg audio, "audio/webm"-webm audio, etc. When playing, browser searches the audio supported by the browser from the top <source> element, and play it when a valid audio is found, and the audio specified by the remaining <source> element will not be found again. In other words, an <audio> element can play at most one audio, even if you use multiple <source> elements. Therefore, it is strongly recommended that you convert the same audio into multiple format files, such as mp3 format, ogg format, wav format, etc., and then specify these format files separately through the <source> element, so that it can be used on as many devices as possible. It may be played on more browsers, because different browsers can play different audio formats.

Look at the example:

```
<audio controls loop>
    <source src="123.mp3" type="audio/mp3">
    <source src="123.ogg" type="audio/ogg">
    <source src="123.wav" type="audio/wav">
    <h2 style="color: red"> Your browser does not support the audio element <h2>
</audio>
```

The browsing effect is the same as the above. The browser will look for playable files in turn, first try 123.mp3, if it fails, try 123.ogg again, if it still fails, try 123.wav again, and report an error if it fails to play.

Some main events of the <audio> element object (used in JS code) are shown in Table 2.1.

Table 2. 1 events of the <audio> element object

event	description
oncanplay	Triggered when the audio resource is ready
onended	Triggered when the playback ends (you can send a message like "Thank you for listening")
onerror	Triggered when an error occurs during file loading
onloadeddata	Triggered when media data has been loaded
onloadedmetadata	Triggered when metadata (such as resolution and duration) is loaded
onpause	Triggered when the media is suspended by the user or the program
onplay	Triggered when starting to play
onplaying	Triggered when the medium has started playing
onreadystatechange	Triggered whenever the ready state changes
ontimeupdate	Triggered when the playback position changes (such as when the user fast-forwards to a different position in the medium)
onvolumechange	Triggers whenever the volume changes (including setting the volume to mute)

In actual web development, the most commonly used events are oncanplay, onended, and onerror. For example, the play button is activated in the oncanplay event to allow the user to click "play" and load the next song in the onended event.

Some of the main attributes of the <audio> element object are (often used in JS programming), see Table 2.2.

Table 2.2 Attributes of the <audio> element object

attributes	description
controller	Returns the MediaController object representing the current media controller of the audio
controls	Set or return whether the audio should display controls (such as play/pause, etc.)
crossOrigin	Set or return the CORS settings of current audio
currentSrc	Returns the URL of the current audio
currentTime	Set or return the current playback position in the audio (in seconds)
duration	Returns the length of the audio (in seconds)
ended	Returns whether the audio playback has ended
error	Returns a MediaError object representing the status of the audio error
loop	Set or return whether the audio should be played again at the end
muted	Set or return whether to turn off the sound
paused	Set or return whether the audio is paused
playbackRate	Sets or returns the speed of audio playback. 1.0 normal, 2.0 2 times speed, 0.5 half speed, -1.0 backward
played	Returns a TimeRanges object representing the played part of the audio
preload	Sets or returns the value of the preload attribute of the audio
readyState	Returns the current ready state of the audio
src	Sets or returns the value of the src attribute of the audio
volume	Set or return the audio volume, the value range is [0, 1], the default value is 0.5, 0 means mute

The main methods of the <audio> element object are shown in Table 2.3.

Table 2.3 Methods of the <audio> element object

Method	Description
load()	Reload audio element
play()	Start playing audio
pause()	Pause the currently playing audio

Using these properties, events and methods, it is easy to develop a web player using JS language. Next, we will implement the audio player shown in Figure 2.2.

Music: Beijing Beijing

Figure 2.2 A simple audio player

Instead of the playback controls provided by the <audio> element, we use JS programming to control the playback and pause of the music. The implemented code is as follows:

```html
<!DOCTYPE html>
<html>

<head>
    <meta charset="utf-8">
    <title>music player</title>
</head>

<body>
    <p> Music: Beijing Beijing </p>
    <audio src="beijing.mp3" id="audio" oncanplay="myready()" onended="myend()"> Audio element is not
supported </audio>
    <input type="range" id="progress" style="width:300px" value="0" onchange="change()"><br>
    <button onclick="myplay()">play</button>
    <button onclick="mypause()">pause</button>
    <button onclick="myloop()">loop</button>

    <script>
        var aud = document.getElementById("audio");
        var pro = document.getElementById("progress");
        var position = 0;
        var timer;

        function myready() {
            pro.max = aud.duration.toFixed(0);
        }
        function change() {
            position = aud.currentTime = pro.value;
        }

        function myend() {
            aud.currentTime = 0;
            clearInterval(timer);
            pro.value = 0;
        }

        function myplay() {
            aud.play();
            timer = setInterval(function () {
                position++;
                pro.value = position;
            }, 1000);
        }

        function mypause() {
            clearInterval(timer);
            aud.pause();
        }

        function myloop() {
            aud.loop = !aud.loop;
```

```
        }
    </script>
</body>

</html>
```

A loop timer is used in the code to move the progress bar, and the progress bar is simulated by the range type of <input> element. At the beginning, assign the value of the duration attribute (the total number of audio playback seconds) of the <audio> object to the max attribute of the <input> element, and then add 1 to the value attribute of the <input> element every second, so that the slider keeps moving right, and when it moves to the end, the audio just finished playing. If you drag the slider with the mouse, assign the value of the value attribute of the <input> element to the currentTime attribute of the <audio> element, so that the fast forward or rewind function is realized.

The <audio> element can only perform simple controls such as playback, pause, and stop of audio playback, other complex operations, such as channel merging and splitting, reverberation, pitch, pan control, and audio amplitude compression, etc , You need to use the AudioContext object, see "Chapter 4 Web Audio API" for details.

Practical exercise 1: Add volume control slider based on the above example, just like Figure 2.3.

Figure 2.3 Add volume control slider

Practical exercise 2: Combine the functions of the "Play" and "Pause" buttons, according to Figure 2.4.

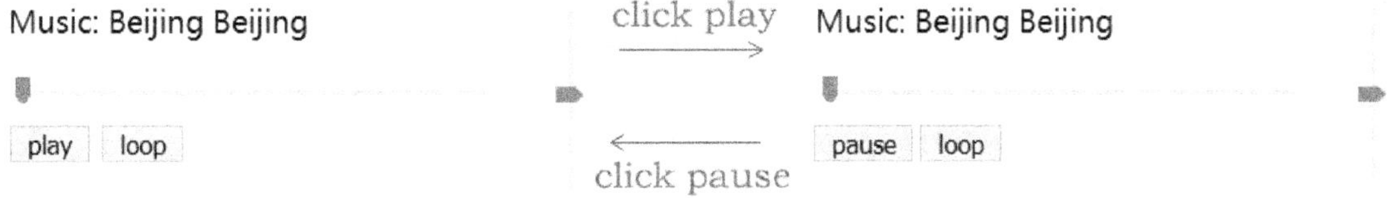

Figure 2.4 Combining the play and pause buttons

2.2 <video> element

The <video> element is used to play video, and its syntax is as follows:

```
<video autoplay controls crossorigin="" loop muted preload="" playsinline="" poster="" src=""
width="" height="" >
     [<source src="" type="">
     <source src="" type="">
     <source src="" type="">
     ......
     Your browser does not support the video element]
</video>
```

Most of the attributes are the same as the <audio> element, but the <video> element allows you to specify the size of the window for video playback. The attribute poster specifies a picture displayed on the playback window when the video is being loaded. It is generally an introduction to the video. The attribute playsinline enables inline playback, which is mainly used on mobile devices. Inline playback means that the playback screen is limited to the <video> element instead of full screen.

Look at the following example:

```
<video src="tobymanley.ogg" controls> The browser does not support the video element </video>
```

The browsing effect is shown in Figure 2.5.

Figure 2.5 The default appearance of the <video> element

The default control buttons are relatively complete, which can play, pause, fast forward and rewind, control the volume, and play in full screen. Let's look at another example:

```
<video width="320" height="240" controls>
  <source src="movie.mp4" type="video/mp4">
  <source src="movie.ogg" type="video/ogg">
  <h1> Your browser does not support the video element</h1>
</video>
```

The size of the playback window is specified as 320*240, and two video format files are specified at the same time. If the browser can support the mp4 format, then the movie.mp4 will be played, otherwise if the ogg format is supported, the movie.ogg will be played. If none is supported, an error will be reported.

The common events and methods of the <video> element are the same as the <audio> element object. The properties of the <video> element object are the same as the <audio> element except for height, width, and poster. For details, please refer to the <audio> in previous section of this book.

The chrome (version 70 or latter) supports the "picture-in-picture" function of the <video> element. The "picture-in-picture" here is not the picture-in-picture of the video in the traditional sense, but the playback picture can be separated from the page. "Floating" on the top of the screen, so that we can work in general while watching the video. Similar to Figure 2.6.

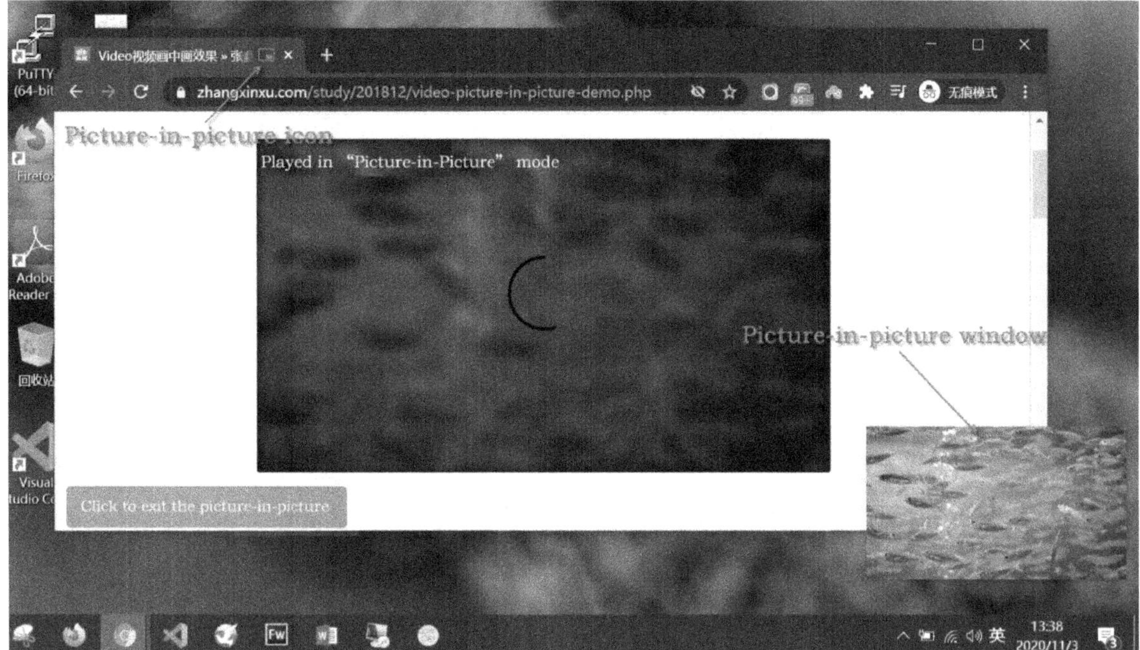

Figure 2.6 Picture in Picture

The general method of implementation is: add a button "enter picture-in-picture", the user clicks the button to call the videoElem.requestPictureInPicture() method, and the button becomes "exit picture-in-picture", when the user clicks the "exit picture-in-picture" button, the document.exitPictureInPicture() method will be called. In addition, the <video> element object adds two events enterpictureinpicture (triggered when entering a picture-in-picture) and leavepictureinpicture (triggered when exiting a picture-in-picture), and a picture-in-picture window object pictureInPictureWindow is added to the actual parameter event of the enterpictureinpicture event handler , The two read-only attributes width and height of this object save the width and height of the picture-in-picture, and the resize event is triggered when the window size is changed. Look at the example:

```html
<body>
  <video id="video" controls playsinline loop src="movie.mp4">
    <h1> Your browser does not support the video element</h1>
  </video><br>
  <input id="togglePipButton" type="button" value="Enter picture-in-picture">
  <script>
    const videoElem = document.getElementById("video");
    const togglePipBtn = document.getElementById("togglePipButton");

    togglePipBtn.hidden = !document.pictureInPictureEnabled || videoElem.disablePictureInPicture;

    togglePipBtn.addEventListener("click", async() => {
      try {
        if (!document.pictureInPictureElement) {
          await videoElem.requestPictureInPicture();
```

```
        } else {
          await document.exitPictureInPicture();
        }
      } catch (err) {
        throw err;
      }
    });

    function enterPinPHandler(event) {
      var pinpWindow = event.pictureInPictureWindow;
      pinpWindow.addEventListener("resize", () => console.log("Changed the size"));
      console.log("Floating window size : ", pinpWindow.width, "*", pinpWindow.height);
    }

    videoElem.addEventListener("enterpictureinpicture", enterPinPHandler);
    videoElem.addEventListener("leavepictureinpicture", () => console.log("Exit picture-in-picture "));
  </script>
</body>
```

"=>" is an arrow function, () => console.log("Changed the size") is equal to function(){console.log("Changed the size");}, please learn about arrow functions of JavaScript language from the Internet or other books.

Practical exercise 1: Refer to the previous <audio> example to design a video player. The effect diagram is shown in Figure 2.7.

Figure 2.7 A simple video player

Practical exercise 2: Combine the "play" and "pause" buttons on the basis of practical exercise 1, as shown in Figure 2.8.

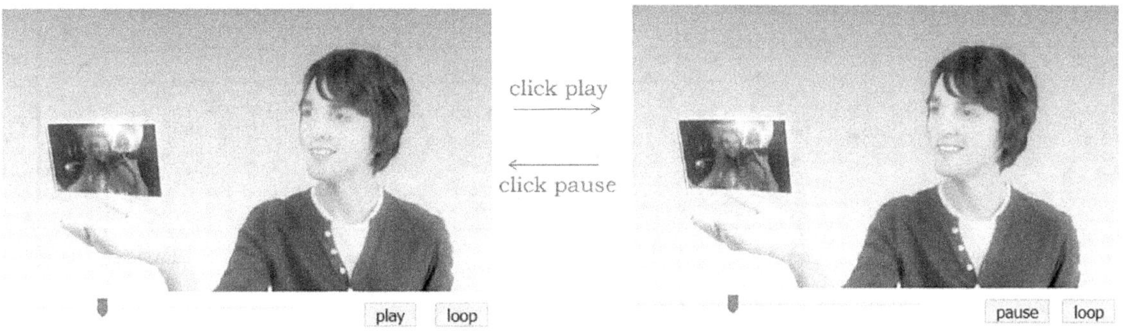

Figure 2.8 Combining play and pause buttons

2.3 <track> element

The <track> element allows you to add subtitles, narration, screen reader descriptions and chapters to the video and audio. In fact, a text track is added. The format of a video is shown in Figure 2.9.

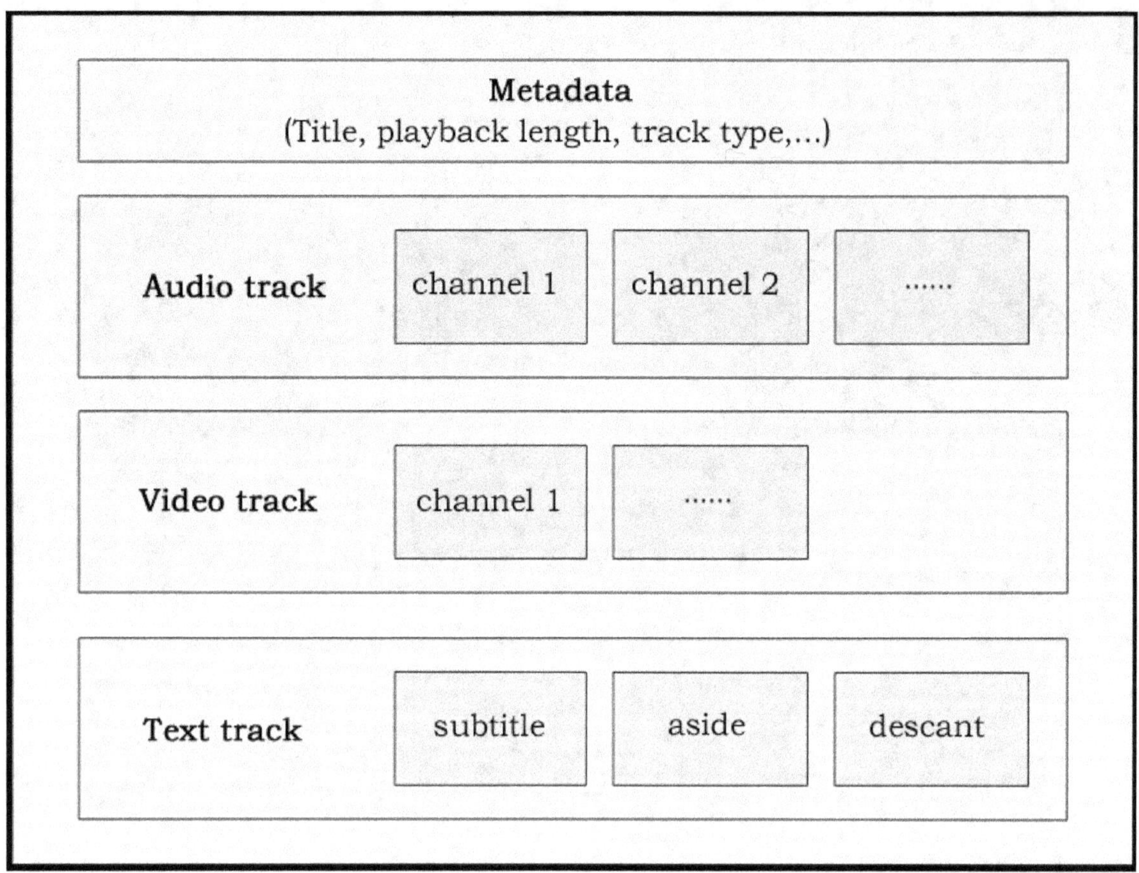

Figure 2.9 Video is composed of tracks

The <track> element can only be used as a child element of the <audio> or <video> element, and can only be arranged after the <source> element. In the same <audio> or <video> element, <track> is allowed to appear multiple times, and is used to specify text tracks in different languages for the user to choose. The syntax of this element is as follows:

```
<track [ label="" kind="" srclang="" default ] src="">
```

label attribute - Define the name of the text track, allowing users to select different text tracks by name, as shown in Figure 2.20.

Figure 2.20 Choose a different text track

If there are multiple <track> elements, only one <track> is allowed to appear "default" attribute (the default text track). If there is no "default", the text track content will not be displayed.

kind attribute - Define the type of text track, its value can be:

subtitles: transcribing or translating human voices into texts in different languages and displayed at the top of video. It's the default value.

captions: mainly for occasions that are difficult to hear (such as deafness, silent media playback or too much noise around), this is the main difference from subtitles.

descriptions: Descriptive text of a scene in a video or drama. Read these texts again through a screen reader to help people who have difficulty viewing (such as blind, driving, or the screen resolution is too low to see clearly).

Chapter: Chapter title, designed to allow users to browse media resources to quickly locate and play. The player will provide a list of chapters for users to choose from.

srclang attribute - Define the language on the text track. Different languages have different codes. For example, common language codes are: en (English), zh (simplified and traditional Chinese), fr (French), ja (Japanese), ru (Russian), es (Spanish), ar (Arabic), etc. For details, search for "ISO language code" by Google. Note, When kind's value is "subtitles", the srclang attribute cannot be omitted.

Let's look at an example:

```
<video controls>
    <source src="movie.mp4" type="video/mp4">
    <track label="中文" src="movie1.vtt" kind="subtitles" srclang="zh" default>
    <track label="English" src="movie2.vtt" kind="subtitles" srclang="en">
</video>
```

In this example, English and Chinese subtitles are provided for users to choose by themselves. The default is Chinese. Put the subtitle files movie1.vtt, movie2.vtt and the video file movie.mp4 in the same directory where the web page file is located (yes, you don't have a subtitle file yet, please refer to the following content to make it yourself), and then browse http://localhost or a domain name like http://www.abc.com (refer to Chapter 1 to build a local web server accessed by domain name), you will see the effect shown in Figure 2.21.

Figure 2.21 Subtitles in two languages

Click the icon to pop up the subtitle language selection box, you can see that the default is Chinese. After clicking play, subtitles will be displayed at the bottom of the video, refer to Figure 2.22.

Figure 2.22 Select Chinese subtitles

Pay attention to the following three aspects when using the <track> element:

1. It can only be accessed through the http:// or https:// protocol. If the file:// protocol is used, the <track> element is invalid.

2. Add a line to the configuration file mime.types of nginx or apache (usually already there):

```
text/vtt        vtt;
```

3. The subtitle file name has the extension of .vtt and is saved in utf-8 encoding. The first line must be WEBVTT, then the first section starting with a blank line (the subtitle file can contain any number of sections), and then the second section starting with a blank line, and so on. The description can appear anywhere, and the number of times is unlimited.

Let's take a look at how to make a subtitle file. The complete format of a subtitle file is shown in Figure 2.23.

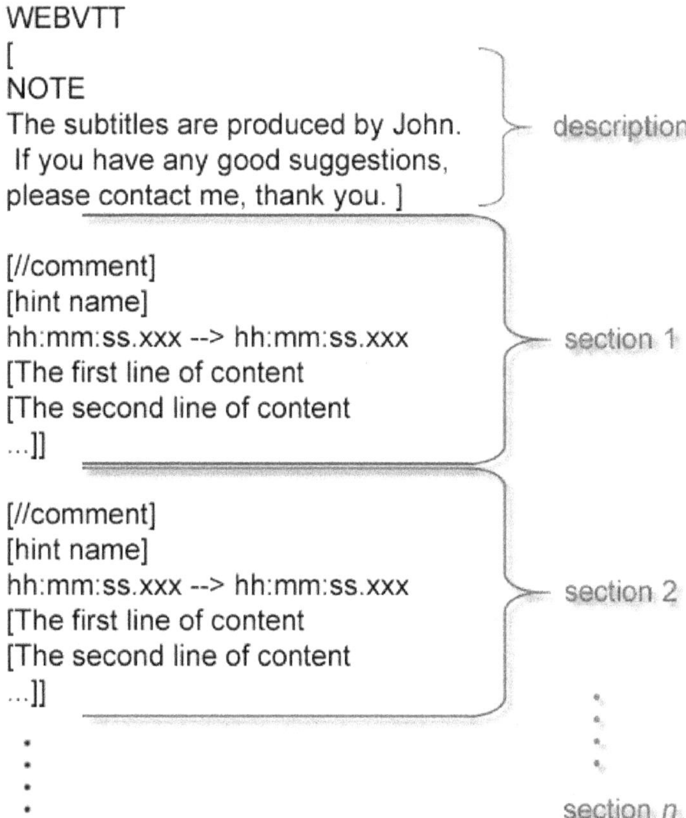

Figure 2.23 Subtitle file format

The part enclosed by square brackets is optional. The time format hh:mm:ss.xxx represents hours, minutes, seconds and microseconds. The first three parts are expressed by two digits, and microseconds are expressed by three digits. The time parts on the left and right sides of "-->" in each section indicate that the content in this section will be displayed at this time period. The content in a section can contain multiple lines. Let's look at a specific example of a subtitle file:

```
WEBVTT

//Alice's lines
Alice
00:00:01.000 --> 00:00:05.000
I don't think so. You?

//John's lines
John
00:00:07.167 --> 00:00:12.042
I'm Ok!
Where are we going?
```

This example tells the browser to display the subtitle "I don't think so. You?" when the video is played from 00:00:01.000 to 00:00:05.000, and when the video is played to 00:00:07.167 to 00:00 :12.042 and two other sentences are displayed. Enter the above content into the Notepad, and then save it as a move.vtt file in utf-8 encoding. Refer to Figure 2.24 for specific operations.

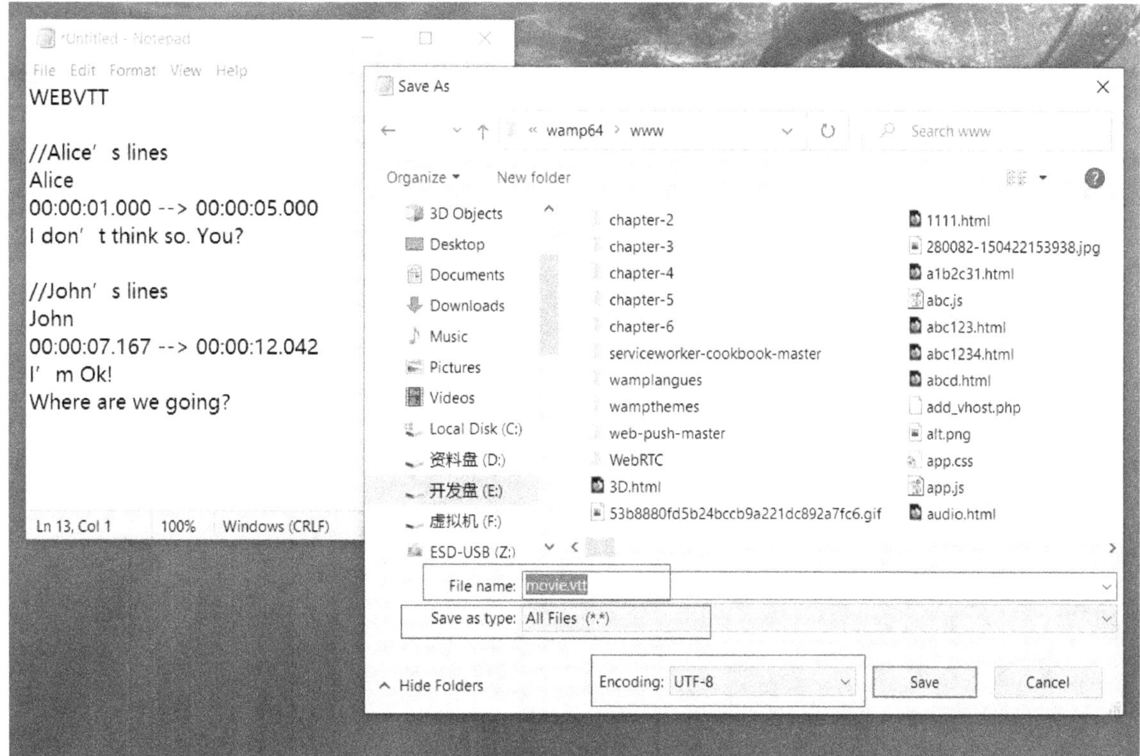

Figure 2.24 Edit subtitle file with Notepad

We can also specify css styles for subtitles. These styles are allowed to be placed in any of three places:

1. In the style sheet of the web page file. Use the ::cue pseudo-class, such as:

```
<style>
  video::cue{
      background-color: transparent;
  }
  …
</style>
```

2. The style sheet of the subtitle file. Use STYLE to guide, such as:

```
WEBVTT

STYLE
::cue {
background-color: rgba(100, 100, 100, 0.4);
color: white;
}

STYLE
::cue(b) {
color: red;
```

```
}

00:00:00.000 --> 00:00:10.000
Hello <b>world</b>.
```

3. In each section of the subtitles. It is written directly after the time period, but the style name is different from the style name of CSS. For detailed introduction, please refer to https://developer.mozilla.org/en-US/docs/Web/API/WebVTT_API.

Finally, we look at a complete example, adding the subtitle file movie.vtt made above to an English movie:

```html
<!DOCTYPE html>
<html>

<head>
  <title>Chinese subtitle</title>
  <style>
    video::cue{
        background-color: rgba(100, 100, 100, 0.5);
        color: white;
    }
  </style>
</head>

<body>
  <video src="tobymanley.ogg" controls>
    <track label="Chinese subtitle" src="movie.vtt" kind="subtitles"
 srclang="zh"
default>
  </video>
</body>

</html>
```

The white subtitle text is displayed on a translucent gray background. Put the subtitle file movie.vtt and the video file tobymanley.ogg in the directory where the web page file is located, and then browse the web page through the http protocol to see the subtitle effect.

Chapter 3

Media Stream

The media stream consists of several video tracks and/or several audio tracks. The video and audio content obtained from multimedia devices (such as microphones, headphones, cameras, etc.) will continuously enter the browser, which is called media source in the browser, just it's like a spring that keeps coming out of water. The MediaStream object can be used to delete and add audio/video tracks from the media stream at will, and the tracks can also be reassembled into various media streams. The video can be played by assigning the video media stream to the srcObject attribute of the <video> element object, and the audio can be played by assigning the audio media stream to the srcObject attribute of the <audio> element object. However, the media objects of some older browsers do not have the srcObject attribute. At this time, the following code can be used to increase the general adaptability of the page.

```
if ('srcObject' in videoElem) {
    videoElem.srcObject = mediaStream;
} else {
    videoElem.src = URL.createObjectURL(mediaStream);
}
```

See Figure 3.1 to further understand the media flow from a global perspective.

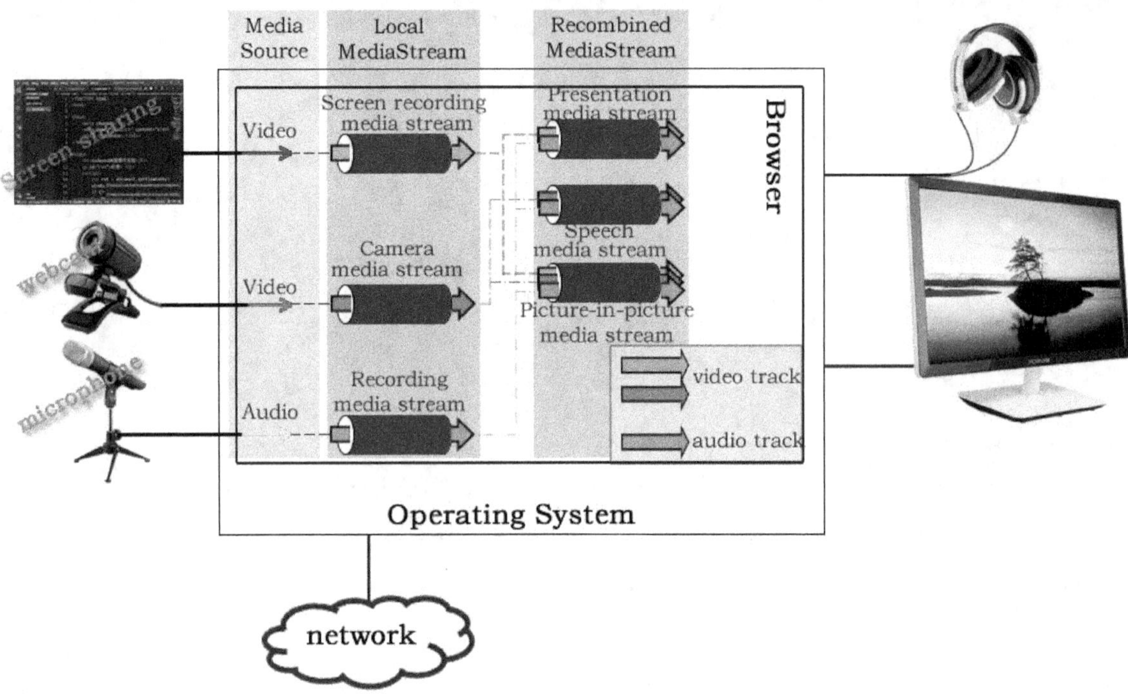

Figure 3.1 Media stream and media equipment

To operate the media stream in the page document, several interface objects such as MediaDevices, MediaStream, MediaStreamTrack, MediaStreamConstraints, and MediaRecorder (optional) are needed.

If the computer does not have a camera and microphone, please install the virtual camera e2eSoft Vcam to facilitate the study in the following chapters.

3.1 MediaDevices Interface

MediaDevices is a child object of navigator, and navigator is a child object of window. The MediaDevices interface obtains media streams from media input devices (such as microphones, cameras, shared screens, etc.), but the browser will pop up a dialog box asking the user whether to allow the browser to operate the multimedia device. MediaDevices has a devicechange event, which is triggered when the connected media device changes (such as plugging in or unplugging a USB microphone). Several methods commonly used by the MediaDevices object are as follows.

1、getUserMedia()

Open the media input device to obtain the media source and return a MediaStream type of media stream. The parameters of the calling method are different, and the audio/video tracks contained in the returned media stream are also different. This method is declared as follows:

```
navigator.mediaDevices.getUserMedia(constraints:MediaStreamConstraints): Promise
```

The formal parameter constraints is used to obtain media tracks that meet the conditions. Its type MediaStreamConstraints is a dictionary. This dictionary has only two attributes, audio and video, whose values are either Boolean or dictionary. Let's see some specific examples, refer to Figure 3.2.

```
const constraint1 = {
    video: true
};
```
Only video track

```
const constraint2 = {
    audio: true
};
```
only audio track

```
const constraint3 = {
    video: true,
    audio: true
};
```
Contain video and audio tracks

```
const constraint4 = {
    audio: true,
    video: {
        width: 1280,
        height: 720
    }
};
```
Contains audio/video tracks, and Video resolution as close as possible 1280*720

```
const constraint5 = {
    audio: {
        sampleSize: 8,           /*8-bit sampling data*/
        echoCancellation: true   /*Echo cancellation*/
    }
    video: {
        facingMode: "user"     /*(Mobile phone) Front camera*/
    }
};
```

```
const constraint6 = {
    video: {
        width: {
            min: 640,        /*Minimum 640*/
            max: 1920,       /*Max 1920*/
            ideal: 1080      /*Best 1080*/
        },
        height: {
            min: 400,
            max: 1200
        }
    },
    audio: {
        sampleSize: 8,
        channelCount: 2,        /*Two-channel*/
        noiseSuppression: true /*Noise reduction*/
    }
};
```

```
const constraint7 = {
    video: {
        facingMode: {
            exact: "environment" /*rear camera*/
        }
        frameRate: {        /*Frames per second*/
            ideal: 10,
            max: 16
        },
        aspectRatio: { ideal: 1.7777777778 }
    },                      Aspect ratio
    audio: {
        channelCount: 2,
        echoCancellation: true,
        autoGainControl: true  /*Turn on auto gain*/
    }
};
```

Figure 3.2 Get different media sources

For audio tracks, there are these additional attributes: latency (double-precision floating point number), sampleRate (sampling frequency), volume (volume, value range [0.0,1.0]). For the video track, there are these additional attributes: facingMode (select the camera, you can also take the value "left"-the camera on the left, "right"-the camera on the right), and "width: 1080" is equivalent to "width: {ideal : 1080 }", but different from "width: {exact: 1080 }", because "exact" means "=" symbol and the former means "≈" symbol. Conditions are used to select media sources, not to set media sources. If the conditions are too strict, there may be no media sources that meet the requirements, although multiple multimedia devices (such as microphones, cameras, etc.) may be connected to the computer.

The getUserMedia() method returns a Promise. When the requested media is successfully obtained, the routine handler will receive the MediaStream object parameters. If the user refuses permission, or the matching media is not available, the error handler will receive a DOMException error object. Let's look at a practical example:

```html
<!DOCTYPE html>
<html>

<head>
    <meta charset="UTF-8">
    <meta name="viewport" content="width=device-width, initial-scale=1.0">
    <title>getUserMedia() method</title>
</head>

<body>
  <video id="vid" autoplay playsinline></video>
<script>
  if (!navigator.mediaDevices || !navigator.mediaDevices.getUserMedia) {
     alert("The getUserMedia() method is not supported!");
     throw 'exit';
  }
  const constraint = {
     audio: {
        echoCancellation: true,
        noiseSuppression: true
     },
     video: true
  }

  function successHandler(stream) {
     var vide = document.getElementById("vid");
     vide.srcObject = stream;
  }

  navigator.mediaDevices.getUserMedia(constraint).then(successHandler).catch(
```

```
      err => console.log(err.name + ": " + err.message)
   );
</script>
<body>

</html>
```

This example obtains local audio/video sources and combines them into a media stream, and finally directs the media stream to the <video> element to play it. The noise reduction and echo cancellation functions are turned on when the audio is collected. In this way, the camera image is captured and displayed on the page.

2、getDisplayMedia()

Screen Recording——Record the screen into a media stream and become a video track in the media stream, thereby realizing screen sharing. This method is declared as follows:

navigator.mediaDevices.getDisplayMedia(constraints ? : MediaStreamConstraints): Promise

The optional parameter *constraints* specifies some requirements of the generated video track. The value format is the same as the parameter of the getUserMedia() method, but if the value of the video attribute is a dictionary, the attribute names inside the dictionary are different, mainly:

cursor - Defines whether the mouse pointer appears in the video track. Possible values are "always" (the mouse pointer is always visible unless the mouse is moved out of the shared area. This is the default value), "motion" (the pointer is only displayed when the mouse is moved), "never" (the mouse pointer does not appear).

displaySurface - It specifies the type of display surface to be captured. Possible values are "application" (including all windows opened by the selected application), "browser" (including only the selected tab on the browser), "monitor" (including the entire screen), "window" (only Contains the selected application window).

logicalSurface - Whether to allow the user to select an interface that is not in the display area, such as a window that is covered, an interface that needs to be scrolled to browse beyond the range, etc.

The getDisplayMedia() method returns a Promise. When the requested media is successfully obtained, it resolves a MediaStream object. Example: Change the method getUserMedia() in the above example to getDisplayMedia(), and the other codes remain unchanged.

3、enumerateDevices()

Enumerate all available multimedia devices, such as microphones, cameras, headsets, etc. The declaration of this method is as follows:

navigator.mediaDevices.enumerateDevices(): Promise

The enumerateDevices() method returns a Promise. When the requested media is successfully obtained, it resolves an array of MediaDeviceInfo objects. Each element in the array represents a media device. The read-only attributes of the MediaDeviceInfo object are: deviceId (the unique identifier of the media device), groupId (group identifier, several media devices belonging to the same physical device belong to the same group, such as a monitor with a built-in camera and microphone), kind (Media device type, the types are "videoinput", "audioinput", "audiooutput"), label (description, such as "External USB Webcam").

The following example lists all media devices supported by this machine in an ordered list:

```html
<!DOCTYPE html>
<html>

<head>
    <meta charset="UTF-8">
    <meta name="viewport" content="width=device-width, initial-scale=1.0">
    <title>Enumerate All Media Devices</title>
</head>

<body>
  <h2> Local multimedia equipment:</h2>
  <ol id="devices"></ol>
  <script>
    if(!navigator.mediaDevices || !navigator.mediaDevices.enumerateDevices){
        console.log("The enumerateDevices() method is not supported!");
        throw "exit";
    }

    navigator.mediaDevices.enumerateDevices()
        .then(devices => {
            var oll = document.getElementById("devices");
            devices.forEach(function (device) {
```

```
        let li = document.createElement("li");
        li.innerText = "deviceId: " + device.deviceId + ",  kind: "
+ device.kind + ",  label: " + device.label;
        oll.appendChild(li);
      })
    })
    .catch(function (err) {
      alert(err.name + ": " + err.message);
    });
  </script>
</body>

</html>
```

3.2 MediaStream Interface

MediaStream is the most important interface object used to manipulate media streams in HTML5, such as deleting tracks from the media stream, adding tracks, and creating new media streams. The properties, events, and methods of the MediaStream object are introduced as follows.

1. Attributes

active - Boolean type, true means the media is active. The active media stream indicates that there is an unending track.

ended - Boolean type, true means that all tracks have ended.

id - the unique global id number (uuid).

2. Events

addtrack - Triggered when a track is added.

removetrack - triggered when the track is deleted.

active - Triggered when the media stream is activated.

inactive - Triggered when inactive.

3. Methods

addTrack(track) - Add a track to the media stream, no return value. The parameter track is of type MediaStreamTrack, which represents the added media track.

clone() - Clone the media stream. The cloned media stream has a unique id number.

getAudioTracks() - Get all audio tracks in the media stream and return an array of MediaStreamTrack objects. The audio track is the track whose attribute kind value is "kind".

getVideoTracks() – Get all the video tracks in the media stream and return an array of MediaStreamTrack objects. The video track is the track whose attribute kind value is "video".

getTrackById(id) – Returns the track with the specified id number.

getTracks() – Get all the tracks in the media stream and return an array of MediaStreamTrack objects.

removeTrack(track) - Remove the track from the media stream. The parameter track is of type MediaStreamTrack, which specifies the track to be deleted.

3.3 MediaStreamTrack Interface

The MediaStreamTrack object represents a single media track in a media stream, mainly audio tracks and video tracks, and other tracks include text tracks, image tracks, etc. The properties, events, and methods of this object are described below.

1. Attributes

contentHint - A short description about the type of track content.

enabled - Boolean type, if true, it means normal playback, otherwise the screen is black or muted. If the track is disconnected, you can change the value of this property, but it no longer works. For example, by setting the enabled property of the audio track to realize the on/off "mute" button.

---

id - The uuid of the track, generated by the browser.

isolated - Boolean type. If true, this track is isolated. Once a track is quarantined, the page document cannot access the track. When the RTCPeerConnection.peerIdentity property is set or the track is from a cross-origin, the track will be isolated.

kind - Track type, "audio" means audio track, "video" means video track.

label - Returns the label assigned to the track by a web client (such as a browser) to identify the source of the track, such as "internal microphone". The value of this attribute is allowed to be empty, and it will always be empty as long as no source is connected. If the track is disassociated from its source, the value of the label attribute will no longer change.

muted - Boolean type, true means mute, false means unmute.

readonly - true means that the track content is read-only (such as the source of the video file, or the camera whose settings cannot be changed).

readyState - track state, if the state is "live", it indicates that the real-time media data is streaming in from the source, at this time you can set the enabled property to turn off or on the media data output; if the state is "ended", it indicates that the source is no longer streaming in new media data.

remote - true means the track source is RTCPeerConnection.

2、Events

ended – Triggered when the playback ends, that is, the value of readyState changes to end.

mute – Triggered when the muted property is changed to true. At this time, the track no longer provides data.

isolationchange - Triggered whenever the value of the isolated attribute changes.

unmute - Triggered when the muted property is changed to false.

3、Methods

applyConstraints([constraints]) - Impose several constraints on the track (such as frames per second, echo cancellation, resolution, etc.) to meet the media presentation preferences of the page or app. The optional parameter constraints define specific restrictions, please refer to the introduction of the parameter with the same name in the getUserMedia() method. The restriction items that do not appear in the parameter constraints are restored to their default values, so if the parameter constraints are omitted, all restriction items are restored to their default values. This method returns a Promise, if the restriction is successfully imposed, resolve, otherwise reject. Look at the example:

```javascript
const constraints = {
    width: { min: 640, ideal: 1280 },
    height: { min: 480, ideal: 720 },
    advanced: [
                { width: 1920, height: 1280 },
                { aspectRatio: 1.333 }
        ]
};

navigator.mediaDevices.getUserMedia({ video: true })
.then(mediaStream => {
    const track = mediaStream.getVideoTracks()[0];
    track.applyConstraints(constraints)
    .then(() => {
        console.log("success!");
    })
    .catch(e => {
        console.log("failed@");
        });
});
```

clone() - Clone the track, the new track is the same except for the different id.

getCapabilities() – Get the configuration parameters that can be changed. Returns a MediaTrackCapabilities object, indicating the value range of each property that can be changed. Note that if this method is called on different platforms and different web clients, the returned value may be different. Once you know which restrictions are allowed, you can call the applyConstraints() method to impose specific restrictions.

getConstraints() – returns a MediaTrackConstraints object, which contains the constraints recently imposed by the track. The following function is used to select the front or rear camera, which is specified by the parameter camera.

```
function switchCameras(track, camera) {
    const constraints = track.getConstraints();
    constraints.facingMode = camera;
    track.applyConstraints(constraints);
}
```

getSettings() - Returns a MediaTrackSettings object, which contains all the restrictions currently in effect on the track. Refer to Figure 3.3.

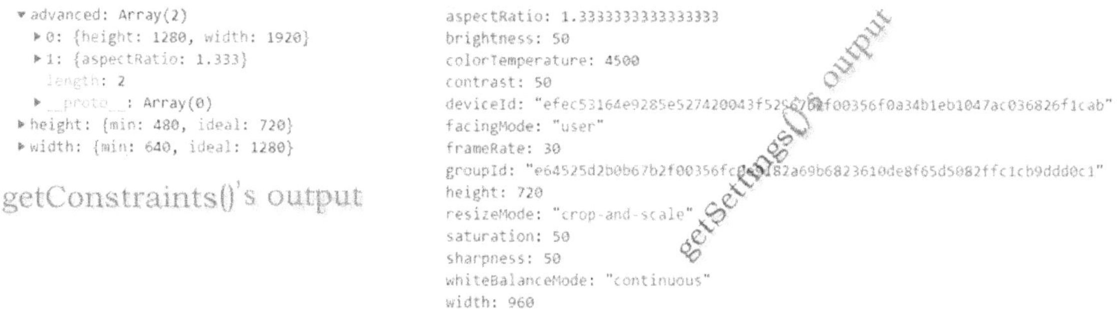

```
▼ advanced: Array(2)                       aspectRatio: 1.3333333333333333
  ▶ 0: {height: 1280, width: 1920}         brightness: 50
  ▶ 1: {aspectRatio: 1.333}                colorTemperature: 4500
    length: 2                              contrast: 50
  ▶ __proto__: Array(0)                    deviceId: "efec53164e9285e527420043f52567b2f00356f0a34b1eb1047ac036826f1cab"
  ▶ height: {min: 480, ideal: 720}         facingMode: "user"
  ▶ width: {min: 640, ideal: 1280}         frameRate: 30
                                           groupId: "e64525d2b0b67b2f00356fcp1e182a69b6823610de8f65d5082ffc1cb9ddd0c1"
getConstraints()'s output                  height: 720
                                           resizeMode: "crop-and-scale"
                                           saturation: 50
                                           sharpness: 50
                                           whiteBalanceMode: "continuous"
                                           width: 960
```


Figure 3.3 The output of the getConstraints() and getSettings() methods

stop() - Stop the media track, it means that this track no longer needs media source, but it does not mean that the corresponding media source is stopped, because other tracks may still use this media source. When all tracks of a media source are stopped , the media source is stopped. Once the stop() method is called, the value of the readyState attribute is set to "ended", and the ended event is triggered at the same time. The following function stops playing the video (the videoElem parameter is the <video> element object)

```
function stopStreamedVideo(videoElem) {
    const tracks = videoElem.srcObject.getTracks();
    tracks.forEach( track => track.stop() );
    videoElem.srcObject = null;
}
```

Finally, let's look at a comprehensive example to realize the media flow in the graph at the beginning of this section, and the browsing effect (click the "Speech" button) as shown in Figure 3.4.

Figure 3.4 Examples of media streams

The complete code is as follows:

```
<!DOCTYPE html>
<html>

<head>
    <meta charset="UTF-8">
    <meta name="viewport" content="width=device-width, initial-scale=1.0">
    <title>media streaming (comprehensive example)</title>
    <style>
        body {
            font-size: 1.5rem;
        }

        #container {
            width: 80%;
            margin: 10 auto;
            height: 96vh;
            text-align: center;
        }

        #box {
            width: 100%;
            border: 1px solid grey;
            background-color: #EEE;
            height: 86vh;
        }

        p {
            text-align: center;
```

```html
        }
    </style>
</head>

<body>
    <div id="container">
        <div id="box">
            <video id="vide" autoplay playinline>The browser does not support the video element!</video>
        </div>
        <p>
            <button id="speech">Speech</button>
            <button id="demo">Demonstrate</button>
            <button id="pinp">Picture-in-picture</button>
            <button id="stop">Stop</button>
        </p>
    </div>

    <script>
        if (!navigator.mediaDevices || !navigator.mediaDevices.getUserMedia) {
            console.log("getUserMedia() method!");
            throw "exit";
        }

        const videoElem = document.getElementById("vide");

        const speechBtn = document.getElementById("speech");
        const demoBtn = document.getElementById("demo");
        const pinpBtn = document.getElementById("pinp");
        const stopBtn = document.getElementById("stop");

        speechBtn.addEventListener("click", speechHandler);
        demoBtn.addEventListener("click", demoHandler);
        pinpBtn.addEventListener("click", pinpHandler);
        stopBtn.addEventListener("click", stopHandler);

        var localAudioStream, localSpeechStream, localDemoStream;
        var buildDemoVideo, buildSpeechVideo, buildPinpVideo;

        navigator.mediaDevices.getUserMedia({
            audio: {
                echoCancellation: true,
                noiseSuppression: true,
                autoGainControl: true
            }
        }).then(audioStream => localAudioStream = audioStream).catch(error => {
            console.log("Error getting audio media stream!");
            throw error;
        });

        navigator.mediaDevices.getUserMedia({
            video: true
```

```javascript
            }).then(videoStream => localSpeechStream = videoStream).catch(error => {
                console.log("Error obtaining camera video media stream!");
                throw error;
            });

            navigator.mediaDevices.getDisplayMedia({
                video: true
            }).then(demoStream => localDemoStream = demoStream).catch(error => {
                console.log("Error getting the shared screen video media stream!");
                throw error;
            });

            var done = setInterval(doWork, 1000);

            function doWork() {
                if (localDemoStream == null || localAudioStream == null || localSpeechStream == null) {
                    return;
                }
                //Presentation media stream
                buildDemoVideo = new MediaStream([...localAudioStream.getAudioTracks(),
...localDemoStream.getVideoTracks() ]);

                //Speech media stream
                buildSpeechVideo = localAudioStream.clone();
                buildSpeechVideo.addTrack(localSpeechStream.getVideoTracks()[0]);

                //Picture-in-picture media streaming
                let tracks = [...localAudioStream.getAudioTracks(), ...localSpeechStream.getVideoTracks(),
...localDemoStream.getVideoTracks() ];
                buildPinpVideo = new MediaStream(tracks);
                clearInterval(done);
            }

            function speechHandler() {
                videoElem.srcObject = buildSpeechVideo;
            }

            function demoHandler() {
                videoElem.srcObject = buildDemoVideo;
            }

            function pinpHandler() {
                videoElem.srcObject = buildPinpVideo;
            }

            function stopHandler() {
                const tracks = videoElem.srcObject.getTracks();
                tracks.forEach(track => track.stop());
                videoElem.srcObject = null;
            }
        </script>
```

```
</body>

</html>
```

However, currently the HTML5 <video> element does not support the playback of picture-in-picture videos (multiple video tracks).

3.4 MediaRecorder Interface

The MediaRecorder interface object is used to record media. After recording, it can be played through the <video> or <audio> element, or it can be stored in a file.

First, use the code shown below to produce a MediaRecorder object.

```
var mediaRecorder = new MediaRecorder(stream[, options]);
```

The parameter *stream* of the constructor specifies the media stream to be recorded. *stream*'s type is MediaStream. The media stream can also come from the srcObject attribute of the <audio> or <video> element object, and the captureStream() method of the <canvas> element object. The optional parameter *options* is a dictionary containing the following attributes:

mimeType - Defines the multimedia type, common types are "audio/mpeg" (MP3 audio), "video/mp4" (MPEG-4 video), "video/ogg" (Ogg video), "video/quicktime" (Apple QuickTime) video).

audioBitsPerSecond - The bit rate of the recorded audio.

videoBitsPerSecond - The bit rate of the recorded video.

bitsPerSecond - The bit rate of recording audio and video. The above two attributes take precedence. If this attribute is defined and one of the above two attributes (such as audioBitsPerSecond), then this attribute only affects the other of the above two attributes (such as videoBitsPerSecond).

If the recording bit rate is not specified, the default video is 2.5Mbps, and the audio bit rate is related to the sampling rate and the number of channels. Look at the example:

```
var options = {
    audioBitsPerSecond: 128000,
    videoBitsPerSecond: 2500000,
    mimeType: "video/mp4"
}
var mediaRecorder = new MediaRecorder(stream, options);
```

The properties, events and methods of the MediaRecorder interface object are as follows.

1. Attributes

mineType (read only) - Returns the MIME type.

state (read only) - Returns the current state of the MediaRecorder object, "inactive" (recording has not started or stopped), "recording" (recording) or "paused" (recording has started but paused).

stream (read only) - Returns the recorded media stream.

ignoreMutedMedia - Boolean type, false means still recording even if the media track is muted or black screen. The default is false.

videoBitsPerSecond (read only) - Returns the current video recording bit rate.

audioBitsPerSecond (read only) - Returns the current audio recording bit rate.

2. Events

dataavailable - Triggered with time slice as the cycle. If the time slice parameter is not specified when calling the start() method (start recording), it will be triggered when the entire media stream finishes being recorded. A BlobEvent object is transferred to the event handler, and the data property of BlobEvent object saves the recorded media data, so we can continuously collect the recorded media data and do further processing.

error - Triggered when an error occurs. The error.name property of the parameter object of the event handler defines the error name.

pause - Triggered when recording is paused.

resume - Triggered when recording resumes from the paused state.

start - Triggered when recording starts.

stop - Triggered when the recording ends. There are two situations that will cause the recording to end: one is to call the stop() method, and the other is to terminate the media stream.

3. Methods

pause() - Pause the recording and trigger the pause event at the same time. The state (MediaRecorder.state) is set to "paused".

requestData() - When in the recording state, calling this method will trigger the dataavailable event and create a new Blob object to store the subsequently recorded media data. Calling this method in the non-recording state will cause a DOM InvalidState error.

resume() - Resume recording from the paused state and trigger the resume event at the same time. .

start([timeslice]) - Start recording, trigger the start event, and set the status to "recording". The recorded media data is stored in a Blob object, and the dataavailable event is triggered when one of the following four situations is encountered: (1) The number of milliseconds defined by the timeslice parameter is reached, (2) The requestData() method is called, (3) The media stream is over, and (4) The stop() method is called. In the first two cases, a Blob object will be created to store the subsequently recorded media data.

stop() - To end the recording, the dataavailable and stop events will be triggered successively, and the status will be set to "inactive".

Next, give an example of recording audio, the page effect is shown in Figure 3.5.

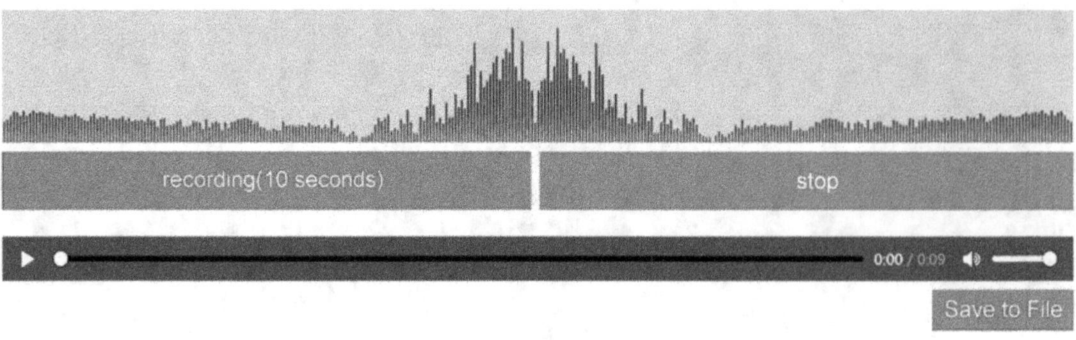

Figure 3.5 web recorder

See the following three files for the code, where index.html is the page file, audio-record.css is the style file, and audio-record.js is the js code program. For the content of audio visualization in the code, please refer to the subsequent section "§4.7 Audio Visualization".

Contents of index.html file:

```html
<!DOCTYPE html>
<html>

<head>
    <meta charset="utf-8">
    <meta name="viewport" content="width=device-width">
    <title>Web dictaphone</title>
    <link href="audio-record.css" rel="stylesheet" type="text/css">
</head>

<body>
    <div class="wrapper">
        <header>
            <h1>Web Recorder</h1>
        </header>

        <section class="maincontainer">
            <canvas class="visualizer" height="120px"></canvas>
            <div id="buttons">
                <button class="record">Record</button>
                <button class="stop">Stop</button>
            </div>
        </section>

        <section class="audiosave">
        </section>
    </div>
    <script src="audio-record.js"></script>
</body>
```

</html>

The content of the audio-record.js file is as follows:

```javascript
const mainSection = document.querySelector('.maincontainer');
const canvas = document.querySelector('.visualizer');
const recordBtn = document.querySelector('.record');
const stopBtn = document.querySelector('.stop');
const soundClips = document.querySelector('.audiosave');
var timeOut, timeCount;
var clipContainer, audio, downloadUrl;

stopBtn.disabled = true;

if (navigator.mediaDevices.getUserMedia) {
    const constraints = { audio: true };

    let onSuccess = function(stream) {
        const mediaRecorder = new MediaRecorder(stream);

        visualize(stream);

        recordBtn.onclick = function() {
            mediaRecorder.start(30000);
            recordBtn.style.background = "red";
            stopBtn.disabled = false;
            recordBtn.disabled = true;
            timeCount = 1;
            timeOut = setInterval(() => {
                recordBtn.textContent = "recording(" + timeCount + "seconds)";
                timeCount++;
            }, 1000);
        }

        stopBtn.onclick = function() {
            mediaRecorder.stop();
            recordBtn.style.background = "";
            recordBtn.style.color = "";
            stopBtn.disabled = true;
            recordBtn.disabled = false;
            clearInterval(timeOut);
            recordBtn.textContent = "Record";
        }

        mediaRecorder.onstop = function(e) {
            if (soundClips.childNodes.length < 2) {
                clipContainer = document.createElement('article');
                audio = document.createElement('audio');
                downloadUrl = document.createElement('a');
                clipContainer.classList.add('clip');
                audio.setAttribute('controls', '');
```

```javascript
                    downloadUrl.textContent = 'Save to file';
                    downloadUrl. className = "downloadurl";

                    clipContainer.appendChild(audio);
                    clipContainer.appendChild(downloadUrl);
                    soundClips.appendChild(clipContainer);

                    audio.controls = true;
                }
            const blob = new Blob(chunks, { 'type': 'audio/mp3' });
            chunks = [];
            const audioURL = URL.createObjectURL(blob);
            downloadUrl.href = audioURL;
            downloadUrl.download = "audioRecordClip.mp3"
            audio.src = audioURL;
        }

        let chunks = [];
        mediaRecorder.ondataavailable = (e) => chunks.push(e.data);
    }


    let onError = (err) => console.log(' The following error occurred:' + err);
    navigator.mediaDevices.getUserMedia(constraints).then(onSuccess, onError);
} else {
    console.log('Your browser does not support the getUserMedia() method!');
}

function visualize(stream) {
    let audioCtx;
    const canvasCtx = canvas.getContext("2d");

    if (!audioCtx) {
        audioCtx = new AudioContext();
    }

    const source = audioCtx.createMediaStreamSource(stream);
    const analyser = audioCtx.createAnalyser();
    analyser.fftSize = 2048;
    const bufferLength = analyser.frequencyBinCount;
    const dataArray = new Uint8Array(bufferLength);

    source.connect(analyser);

    var linear = canvasCtx.createLinearGradient(0, 0, 0, canvas.height);
    linear.addColorStop(0, "red");
    linear.addColorStop(0.7, "blue");
    linear.addColorStop(1, "green");

    draw()

    function draw() {
```

```javascript
    const hWIDTH = canvas.width / 2;
    const HEIGHT = canvas.height;

    requestAnimationFrame(draw);

    analyser.getByteFrequencyData(dataArray);
    canvasCtx.fillStyle = 'rgb(200, 200, 200)';
    canvasCtx.lineWidth = 2;
    canvasCtx.strokeStyle = linear;
    canvasCtx.fillRect(0, 0, canvas.width, HEIGHT);

    canvasCtx.beginPath();

    let step = Math.floor(bufferLength * 3.0 / hWIDTH);
    let x = 0;

    for (let i = 0; i < bufferLength; i = i + step) {
        let y = dataArray[i] * HEIGHT / 256;
        canvasCtx.moveTo(hWIDTH + x, HEIGHT);
        canvasCtx.lineTo(hWIDTH + x, HEIGHT - y);
        canvasCtx.moveTo(hWIDTH - x, HEIGHT);
        canvasCtx.lineTo(hWIDTH - x, HEIGHT - y);
        x += 3;
    }
    canvasCtx.stroke();
  }
}

window.onresize = () => canvas.width = mainSection.offsetWidth;
window.onresize();
```

The content of the audio-record.css file is as follows:

```css
* {
    margin: 0;
    padding: 0;
    box-sizing: border-box;
}

body {
    font-family: 'Helvetica Neue', Helvetica, Arial, sans-serif;
    font-size: 0.8rem;
}

.wrapper {
    height: 100%;
    display: flex;
    flex-direction: column;
}
```

```css
h1,
h2 {
    font-size: 2rem;
    text-align: center;
    font-weight: normal;
    padding: 0.5rem 0 0 0;
}

.maincontainer {
    padding: 0.5rem 0;
}

canvas {
    display: block;
    margin-bottom: 0.5rem;
}

#buttons {
    display: flex;
    flex-direction: row;
    justify-content: space-between;
}

#buttons button {
    font-size: 1rem;
    padding: 1rem;
    width: calc(50% - 0.25rem);
}

button {
    font-size: 1rem;
    background: #0088cc;
    text-align: center;
    color: white;
    border: none;
    transition: all 0.2s;
    padding: 0.5rem;
}

button:hover,
button:focus {
    box-shadow: inset 0px 0px 10px rgba(255, 255, 255, 1);
    background: #0ae;
}

button:active {
    box-shadow: inset 0px 0px 20px rgba(0, 0, 0, 0.5);
    transform: translateY(2px);
}
```

```css
.audiosave {
    flex: 1;
    overflow: auto;
}

section,
article {
    display: block;
}

.clip {
    padding-bottom: 1rem;
}

audio {
    width: 100%;
    display: block;
    margin: 1rem auto 0.5rem;
}

.clip p {
    display: inline-block;
    font-size: 1rem;
}

.clip button {
    font-size: 1rem;
    float: right;
}

.downloadurl {
    background: #f00;
    padding: 0.5rem 0.75rem;
    font-size: 1rem;
    float: right;
    text-decoration: none;
    color: white;
}

@media all and (min-width: 800px) {
    .wrapper {
        width: 90%;
        max-width: 1000px;
        margin: 0 auto;
    }
}
```

Web Audio API

Directly use HTML5 elements <audio> and <video> to play audio/video, we can only do simple controls, such as play, stop, and change the volume. In addition, for some advanced controls, such as pitch shift, reverberation, filtering, delay, compression, equalization, upmixing and downmixing, etc. we can only use the AudioContext interface object. After you are familiar with the native Web Audio Api, in the actual project development, it is recommended to use third-party frameworks, take tone.js for example. Tone.js is used in the music teaching websites https://learningmusic.ableton.com.

Since I will explain various methods of processing audio, such as pitch shifting, reverberation, filtering, equalization, delay, etc., it is necessary for you to understand some music theory first.

Sound - Produced by the vibration of the object, and spread through media such as squeezing the air, and finally reach the ear to drive the tympanic membrane to vibrate, so we hear the sound. The stronger the vibration, the greater the amplitude of the squeezed air, and the louder the sound. If the abscissa represents the time and the ordinate represents the vibration amplitude, then the coordinate system shown in Figure 4.1 can be used to represent a piece of audio.

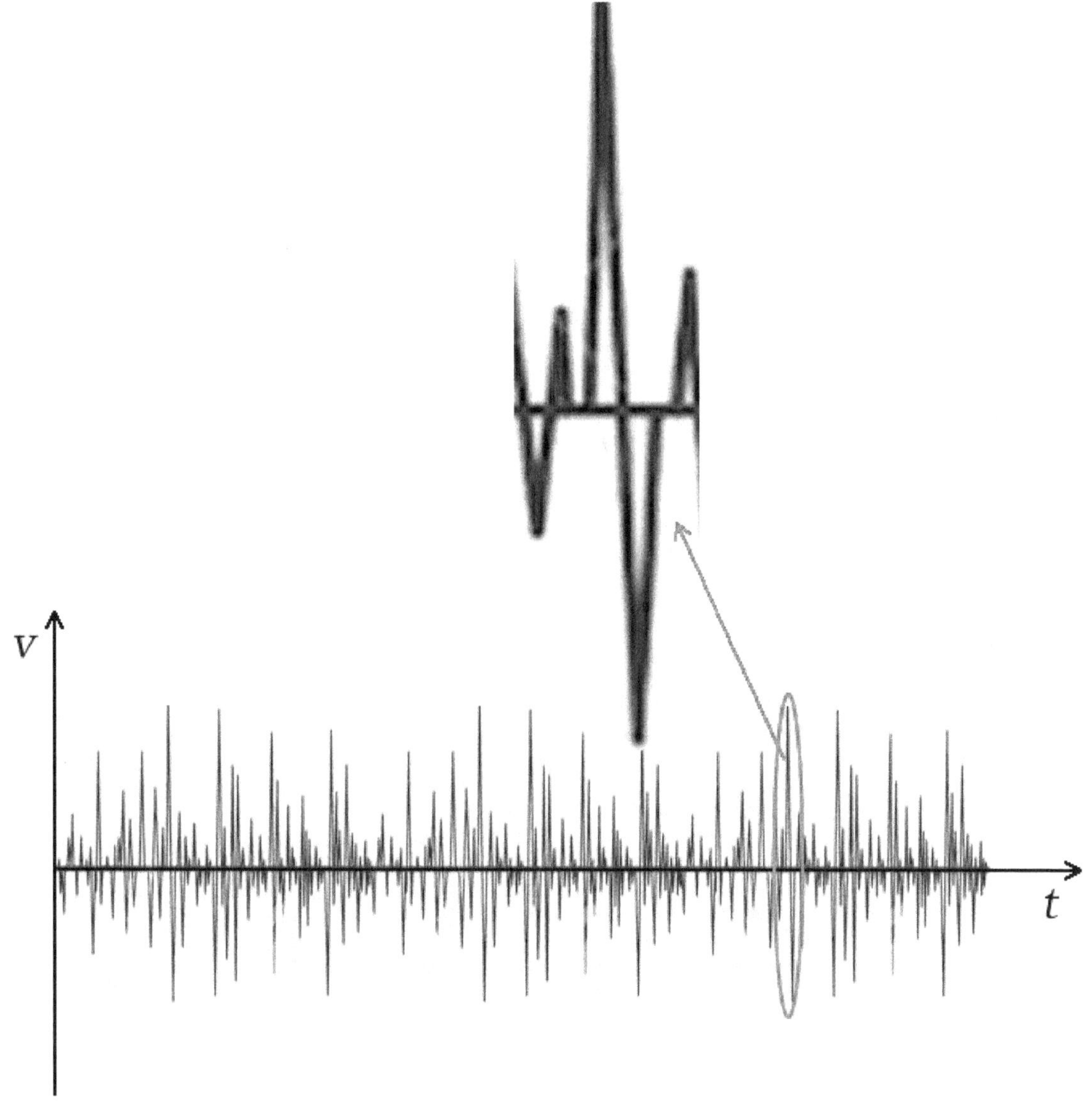

Figure 4.1 A piece of audio

Tone - Closely related to the vibrating "object", such as the human throat, bird's beak, piano, violin, zither, etc. The timbre of the violin and the piano are different, and the timbre is different, the corresponding sound wave waveform is also different. See Figure 4.2.

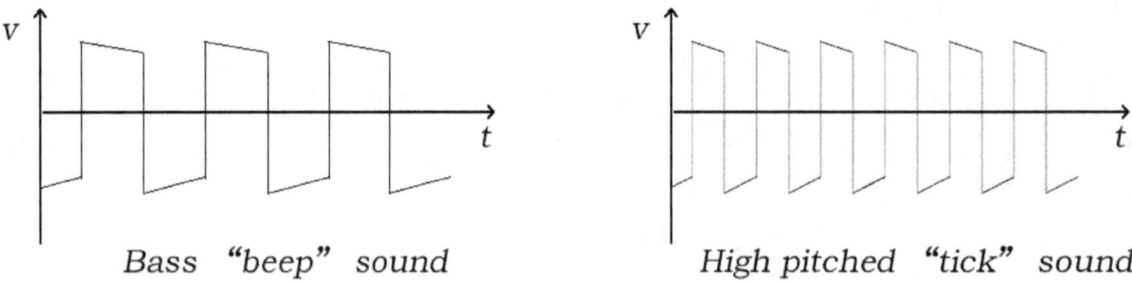

Figure 4.2 The audio waveform determines the tone

Loudness - Also known as volume, is determined by the amplitude of the sound wave, that is, the greater the absolute value of the ordinate in the sound wave coordinate system, the stronger the amplitude, and the louder the sound. The unit of loudness is decibels, the loudness of normal speech is about 50 decibels, and the loudness of yelling is close to 70 decibels. Refer to Figure 4.3.

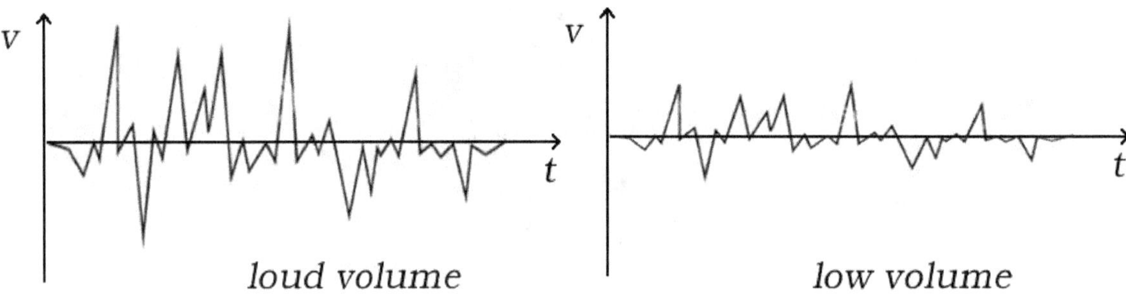

Figure 4.3 Audio amplitude determines the volume

Pitch - Determined by the frequency of the sound wave, the frequency is how many vibrations per second, the unit is Hertz (Hz), for example, 500Hz means 500 vibrations per second. The audible sound frequency range of the human ear is between 20 Hz and 20000 Hz. An octave numbered musical notation scale 1234567i, the corresponding frequency is getting higher and higher, and the frequency of i is exactly twice that of 1, and it is found that the tones with the octave relationship sound similar, such as the three tones of 220Hz, 440Hz, and 880Hz. Although the frequency is very different, but the effect is similar. In the prevailing twelve equal temperament, the two tones (inclusive) that are octave of each other are equally divided into 12 semitones, a total of 1200 cents, that is, one semitone is equal to 100 cents. If the frequency corresponding to 1 of an octave is 260Hz, then the relationship between each numbered musical notation, frequency and centimeter is shown in the lower part of Figure 4.4. Obviously, the frequency range of the lower octave at this time is 130Hz to 260Hz, and the high octave frequency range is between 520Hz and 1040Hz.

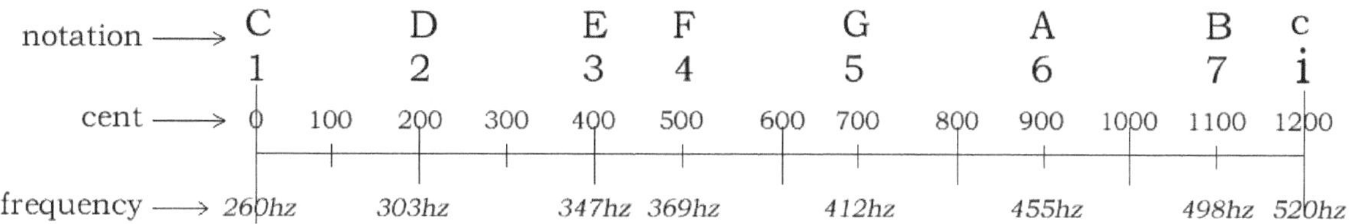

Figure 4.4 Audio frequency determines the pitch

Some English-speaking countries use CDEFGABc instead of the numbered musical notation 1234567i, and the corresponding relationship is shown in the figure above. We often find words like "1=E" and "1=G" in the upper left corner of a numbered musical notation, or mention "E tone" or "G tone" in spoken or written expressions. "1=E" and "E tone" have the same meaning, that is to say that the numbered musical notation 1 has the sound of 3 (because the letter numbered musical notation E is equivalent to the digital numbered musical notation 3), which is equivalent to telling you that 1 should be improved by two whole tones, and 2 should also be raised two whole tones by homeopathy, and so on. Figure 4.5 shows the midrange of the standard keyboard of a piano. The low range on the left and the high range on the right are not drawn. The white keys are full-tones, and the black keys are half a tone apart from the adjacent white keys.

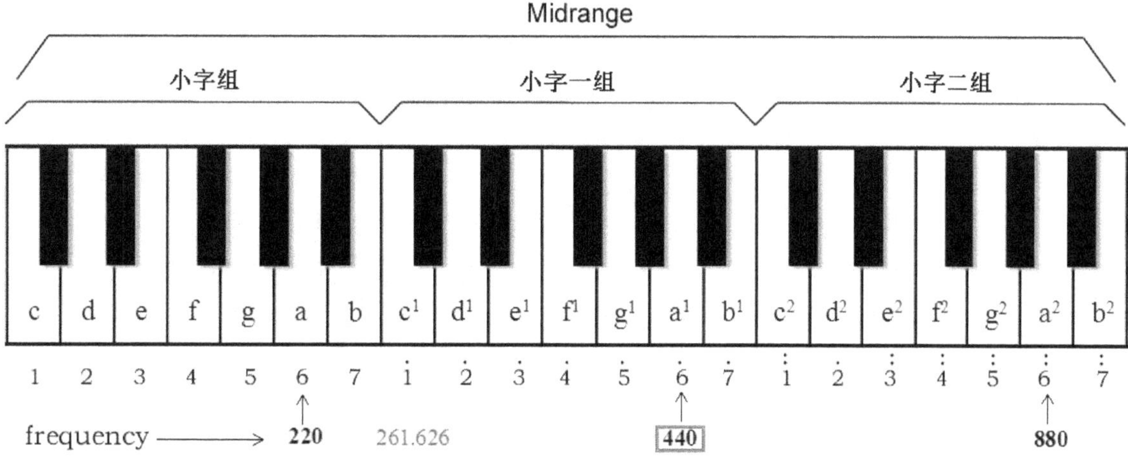

Figure 4.5 The midrange of the piano keyboard

Music - Can easily distinguish the sound of tone and pitch, such as the sound of piano, violin, zither, etc.

Noise - It is difficult to distinguish the pitch and chaotic sounds, such as gongs, drums, explosions, waterfalls, thunder, etc.

Sampling - The amplitude of the object's vibration is continuously changing on the time axis, and appears as a continuous curve in the coordinate system, as shown in Figure 4.6. In order to save the sound in the computer, it is necessary to sample the vibration amplitude v_i at time t_i, such as 0 second amplitude 0, 0.0001 second amplitude 0.001, 0.0002 second amplitude 0.004, ... The number of data recorded per second is called the sampling rate. The sampling rate is generally much greater than the frequency of the sound, otherwise it will be distorted. The higher the sampling rate, the closer to the original sound, but the larger the amount of data. Take the sampling rate of mp3 audio for example, it is 44100Hz, that is, 44100 amplitude data are recorded every second. Figure 4.6 shows that 23 data are sampled in 0.0005 seconds and stored in 4-bit binary, and the sampling rate can be calculated to be 46000 Hz. If each data sampled is saved in 8-bit binary (ie 1 byte), it is called 8-bit audio, if it is saved in 16-bit binary (ie 2 bytes), it is called 16-bit audio, currently 16-bit Audio is mainstream. The more the number of bits, the closer the sampling point is to the sound wave curve, so the sound is more fidelity. For example, 16-bit binary can store any number between -32768 and +32767.

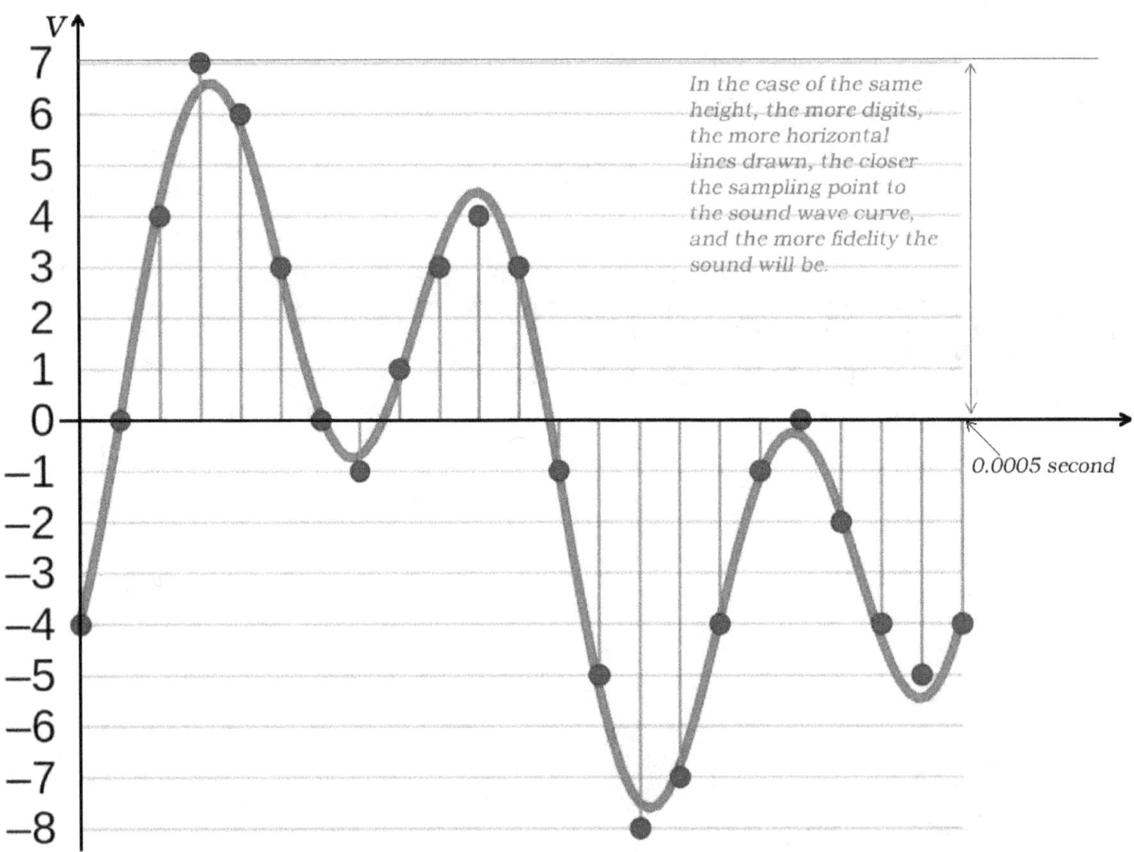

For the example shown in Figure 4.6, the final sampled data is -4, 0, 4, 7, 6, 3, 0, -1, 1, 3, 4, 3, -1, -5, -8, -7, -4 , -1, 0, -2, -4, -5, -4.

Audio FFT - Fast Fourier Transmit (Fast Fourier Transmit), according to the Fourier theory: any sound wave can be broken down into countless sine waves of different frequencies (0 to ∞), different phases and different amplitudes, see As shown in Figure 4.7.

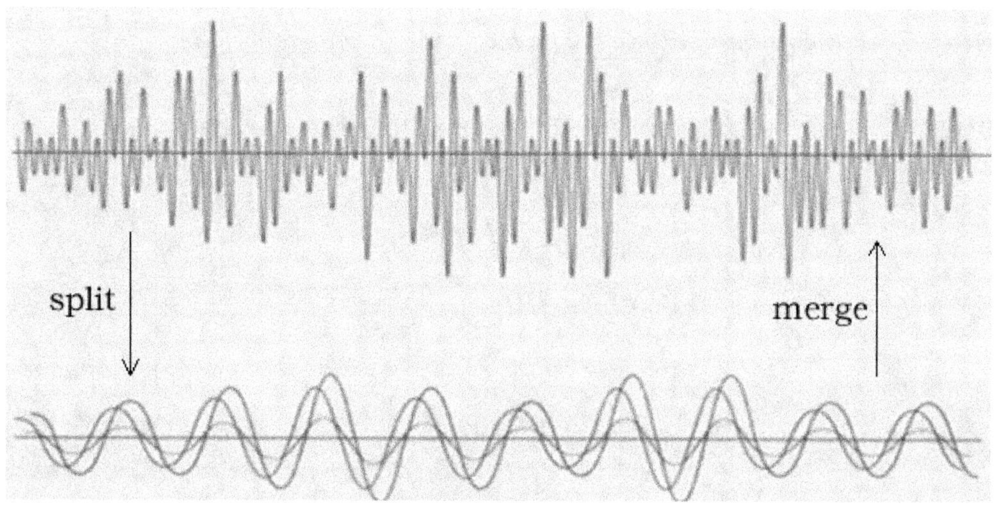

Figure 4.7 Audio Fast Fourier Transform

After disassembly, you can remove sine waves of certain frequencies (called filtering), or adjust the amplitude of certain sine waves (called equalization), but there is no need to increase the sine wave, because the sound wave itself contains sine waves of any frequency. Since the computer can only process discrete data and cannot do infinite Fourier transform, it can only disassemble sine waves with a limited frequency on the computer. The number of sine waves that can be disassembled is the number of sine waves used for each Fourier transform. Half of the number of sampled data. For example, the sampling frequency is 44100Hz, and each FFT uses 2048 sampling data, then only 1024 sine waves of different frequencies can be disassembled, and the frequency of FFT processing is $\lfloor 44100/2048 \rfloor = 21$Hz, that is, finishing one FFT takes about 46 milliseconds $(1/21 \approx 46)$, and the frequency of the i-th sine wave that is disassembled is $i \times 21$ Hz. Refer to Figure 4.8.

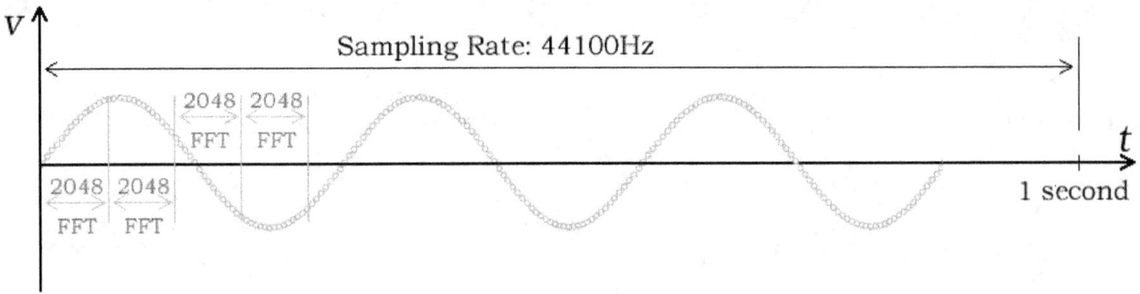

Figure 4.8 FFT schematic diagram

Dry sound - The original sound recorded directly without post-processing.

Wet sound - The sound after post-processing (reverberation, modulation, compression, speed change, etc.).

4.2 AudioContext Object

The AudioContext object is similar to a audio recording studio. It creates various input nodes to receive corresponding audio sources. These audio sources can come from microphones, media streams, audio files, and oscillators (sound waves of a given frequency generated by JavaScript programming). It creates several processing nodes to generate various sound effects such as delay, filtering, mixing, etc. It also creates several output nodes to send the processed audio to different destinations, such as speakers, media streams (subsequent media streams can be added to RTCPeerConnection or saved to the file) and so on. Each node created by AudoContext has several input ports and several output ports. The output port of one node is connected to the input port of another node (using the connect() method of the node object) to form a directed graph of audio processing. See some examples shown in Figure 4.9.

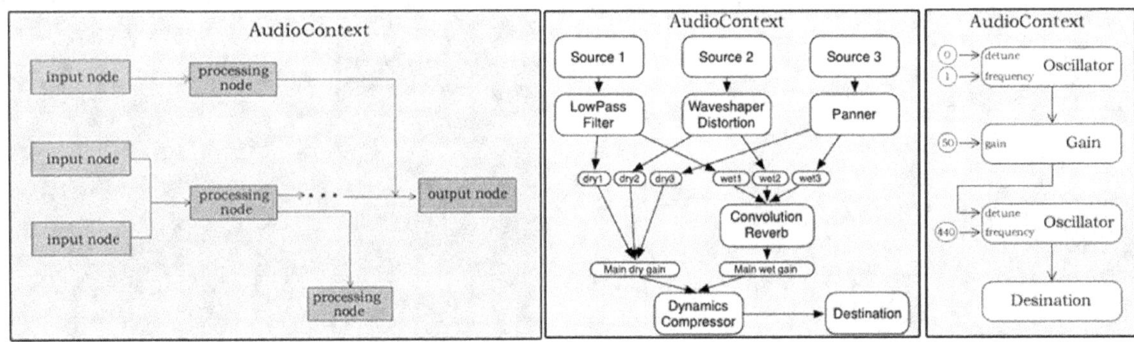

Figure 4.9 Audio processing directed graph

Dry1, dry2, dry3, wet1, wet2, wet3, are all GainNode nodes (volume p table.

An audio processing directed graph a simple player means that the inpu does not necessarily exist an output time volume in a graphical

Table 4.

type	name	object type	Instantiate (The default is the method of AudioContext)	Number of inputs	Number of outputs	Channel count mode	Channel count	Channel interpretation	comments
input node	Oscillator	OscillatorNode	.createOscillator()	0	1	max	2	speakers	A sound wave of a given frequency generated by JavaScript programming
	AudioBufferSource	AudioBufferSourceNode	.createBufferSource()	0	1		defined by the audio source		A piece of decoded audio stored in memory
	MediaElementAudioSource	MediaElementAudioSourceNode	.createMediaElementSource()	0	1				Audio from the <audio> or <video> element
	MediaStreamAudioSource	MediaStreamAudioSourceNode	.createMediaStreamSource()	0	1				Media stream from WebRTC or microphone
	MediaStreamTrackAudioSource	MediaStreamTrackAudioSourceNode	.createMediaStreamTrackSource()	0	1				Media streaming track from WebRTC or microphone
	ConstantSource	ConstantSourceNode	.createConstantSource()	0	1				Output fixed value
processing node	Analyser	AnalyserNode	.createAnalyser()	1	1	max	2	speakers	Real-time visual analysis in time or frequency domain
	AudioWorklet	AudioWorkletNode	new AudioWorkletNode()						Nodes processed in AudioWorkletProcessor
	BiquadFilter	BiquadFilterNode	.createBiquadFilter()	1	1	max	2	speakers	Often used to filter frequency bands
	ChannelMerger	ChannelMergerNode	.createChannelMerger()	variable; default to 6	1	max	2	speakers	Combine multiple channels into one
	ChannelSplitter	ChannelSplitterNode	.createChannelSplitter()	1	variable; default to 6	explicit	Fixed to the number of outputs	discrete	Split one channel into multiple
	Convolver	ConvolverNode	.createConvolver()	1	1	clamped-max	1,2 or 4	speakers	performs a Linear Convolution on a given AudioBuffer
	Delayer	DelayNode	.createDelay()	1	1	max	2	speakers	Delay the input before output
	DynamicsCompressor	DynamicsCompressorNode	.createDynamicsCompressor()	1	1	clamped-max	2	speakers	Provides a compression effect to reduce the volume of the loudest part of the signal
	Gainer	GainNode	.createGain()	1	1	max	2	speakers	change volume
	IIRFilter	IIRFilterNode	.createIIRFilter()	1	1	max	Same as on the input	speakers	can be used to implement tone control devices and graphic equalizers as well
	Panner	PannerNode	.createPanner()	1	1	clamped-max	2	speakers	The location and behavior of the audio source signal in space
	StereoPanner	StereoPannerNode	.createStereoPanner()	1	1	clamped-max	2	speakers	Change the position of the sound source to the left or right
	WaveShaper	WaveShaperNode	.createWaveShaper()	1	1	max	2	speakers	Use curves to apply waveform distortion to the signal
output node	AudioDestination	AudioDestinationNode	.destination	1	0	explicit	2	speakers	Play sound through the speaker
	MediaStreamAudioDestination	MediaStreamAudioDestinationNode	.createMediaStreamDestination()	1	0	explicit	2	speakers	MediaStream with only one track. it can be added to the WebRTC link later.

4.3 AudioNode Object

All audio node objects inherit the AudioNode, so these nodes all have the properties and methods of the AudioNode object. We first introduce the AudioNode, some of its main properties and methods are:

numberOfInputs - The number of input ports. The number of input ports of the input nodes is 0.

numberOfOutputs - The number of output ports. The number of output ports of the output nodes is 0.

channelCountMode - Determines how to calculate the number of channels when upmixing and/or downmixing the input of the node. This attribute has no meaning on nodes without input. Possible values are "max"-equal to the maximum number of channels in all links connected to the same input port; "clamped-max"-ie clamp(0, channelCount, max). Assuming that the maximum number of channels in all input links is x, if channelCount is greater than x, then the final number of channels is equal to x, otherwise it is equal to channelCount; "explicit"-the final channel number is equal to channelCount. For example, in Figure 4.10: if channelCountMode="max", the final channel number of the first input = 4, if it is "clamped-max" or "explicit", the final channel number is equal to 2.

channelCount - The number of channels used for upmixing and downmixing, the default is 2. The final output channel number is also related to the channelCountMode and channelInterpretation properties.

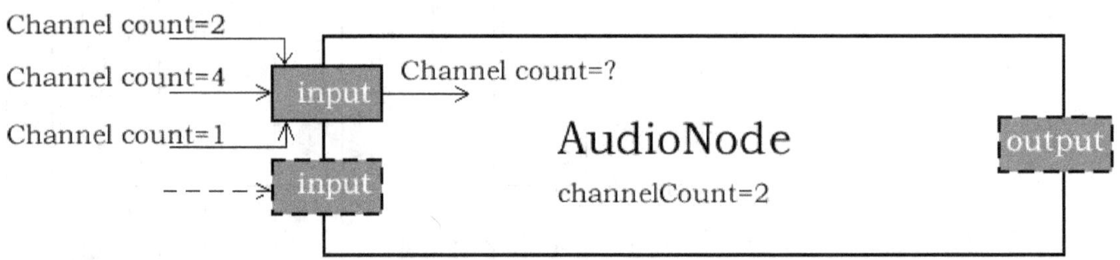

Figure 4.10 Properties of the AudioNode object

channelInterpretation - Defines upmixing and downmixing strategies. This attribute has no meaning on nodes without input. Upmixing occurs when the number of input channels is less than the number of output channels, otherwise downmixing occurs. This attribute can take the value "discrete" (input/output corresponds to channel number one to one, redundant output channels are muted or redundant input channels are ignored), the upmix and downmix operations defined by the "speakers" strategy are shown in the table 4.2.

Table 4.2 Upmix/downmix strategy

Number of input channels	Number of output channels	Upmix/downmix strategy
Mono	Two-channel	Upmix - The mono channel is copied to the left and right channel, namely: output.L = input.M, output.R = input.M
	4 channels	Upmix - The mono channel is copied to the left and right channels, and the left and right surround channels are muted, namely: output.L = input.M, output.R = input.M, output.SL = 0, output.SR = 0
	6 channels (5.1)	Upmix - The mono channel is copied to the center channel, and the other output channels are muted, namely: output.C = input.M, output.RL= output.R = ioutput.SL = output.SR = output.LFE = 0
Two-channel	Mono	Downmix——The output channel is the average value of the input left and right channels, namely: output.M = 0.5 * (input.L + input.R)
	4 channels	Upmix - One-to-one correspondence between the left and right channels, and the left and right surround channels are muted
	6 channels (5.1)	Upmix - One-to-one correspondence between left and right channels, other channels are muted
4 channels	Mono	Down-mix from quad to mono. Downmix - The output channel is the average value of the input four channels, namely: output.M = 0.25 * (input.L + input.R + input.SL + input.SR)
	Two-channel	Downmix-The output left channel is the average value of the input left channel and the left surround channel, and the output right channel is the average value of the input right channel and the right surround channel, namely: output.L = 0.5 * (input.L + input.SL), output.R = 0.5 * (input.R + input.SR)
	6 channels	Upmix - One-to-one correspondence between left and

	(5.1)	right channels and surround channels, and the output center and subwoofer are muted
6 channels (5.1)	Mono	Downmix - The calculation formula is: output.M = 0.7071 * (input.L + input.R) + input.C + 0.5 * (input.SL + input.SR)
	Two-channel	Downmix - The calculation formula is: output.L = input.L + 0.7071 * (input.C + input.SL) output.R = input.R + 0.7071 * (input.C + input.SR)
	4 channels	Downmix - The calculation formula is as follows: output.L = input.L + 0.7071 * input.C output.R = input.R + 0.7071 * input.C output.SL = input.SL output.SR = input.SR
Others		Input/output correspond one-to-one by channel number, redundant output channels are muted or redundant input channels are ignored.

connect(destination[, outputIndex, inputIndex]) – The output of this node is connected to the target (specified by the parameter *destination*). If the target is another node, the audio flows into the input port of that node, and if the target is an instance of the AudioParam interface, then the output of this node is used to change the value of that instance in real time (for example, GainNode.gain is to change the volume in real time). The optional parameters *outputIndex* and *inputIndex* specify the output port number of the node and the input port number of the target node, because a node may have multiple output ports and input ports. If the target is a node, then this method returns the target node, so that it is convenient for us to write this code to connect multiple nodes in series at once, like this: x.connect(y).connect(z)........ If the target is AudioParam, this method does not return.

disconnect([destination, outputIndex, inputIndex]) – Disconnect the link. The meaning of the three parameters is the same as the parameters of the connect() method. If all parameters are omitted, the connections established between all output ports of this node and the target will be disconnected. The allowed combinations of parameters are (destination), (outputIndex), (destination, outputIndex), (destination, outputIndex, inputIndex).

Below we start from the simplest audio processing directed graph to introduce various popular sound effect nodes.

This directed graph has only input nodes and output nodes. Because the local music file is played directly, the AudioContext.createBufferSource() method is used to create an input node of type AudioBufferSourceNode, and the output node is the speaker, that is, the AudioContext.destination node. Refer to Figure 4.11.

Figure 4.11 AudioBufferSourceNode node

The input node of the AudioBufferSourceNode type has no input port, only one output port. It directly streams the decoded audio stored in the attribute *buffer* to the output port in time sequence. The number of channels of the output port is determined by the decoded audio of the buffer. Once the decoded audio data stream in the buffer is exhausted, AudioBufferSourceNode will be automatically destroyed, so if you want to play multiple audio, you must instantiate the AudioBufferSourceNode object multiple times, as shown in Figure 4.12.

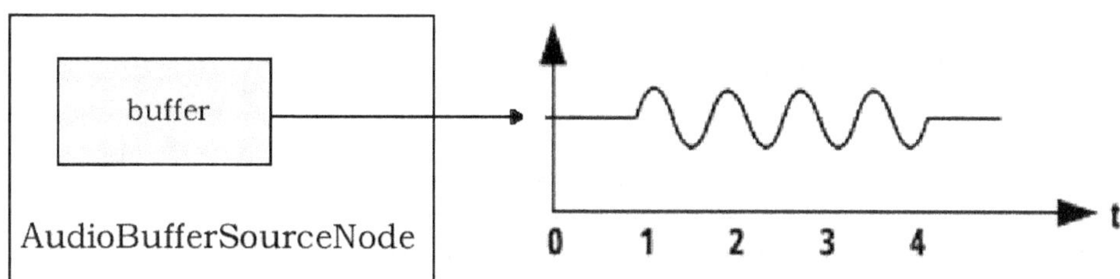

Figure 4.12 AudioBufferSourceNode node description

Since the audio data stored in the music file is non-decoded, we need to use the AudioContext.decodeAudioData() method to decode the non-decoded audio read from the file, then assign the decoded audio data to AudioBufferSourceNode.buffer, and finally call AudioBufferSourceNode.start() method to play. The properties and methods of the AudioBufferSourceNode object are introduced as follows:

buffer – Its type is AudioBuffer, which stores the decoded audio data to be played. If the value is set to null, it means mute mono.

detune - Its type is AudioParam, used to adjust the pitch, the unit is cent, the default is 0. For example, detune.value=100 means to increase a semitone, -100 to decrease a semitone, and 1200 to increase an octave.

loop - If it is true, the audio will be played in a loop, the default is false.

loopStart - Its type is a floating point number, the unit is second, it defines the starting point of each loop, and the default is 0.

loopEnd - Its type is a floating point number, the unit is second, which defines the end of each loop, the default is 0 (there is only 0 seconds to the end of the song).

playbackRate - Its type is AudioParam, which defines the playback rate, and the default is 1.0 (normal speed). For example, playblackRate.value=0.5 means half speed, and 2.0 means double speed.

start() - Call this method to start playing audio.

stop() - Stop playing.

The AudioContext.decodeAudioData(ArrayBuffer, successCallback, errorCallback) method is to decode the non-decoded audio stored in the ArrayBuffer. If the decoding is successful, call the sucessCallback(buffer) function, where the parameter *buffer* contains the decoded audio data. If decoding fails, then call errorCallback(error), where error.err saves the reason for the failure. DecodeAudioData() method can also be written in Promise style: decodeAudioData(ArrayBuffer).then().catch(), refer to the following example for details.

Here is the complete example:

```
<!DOCTYPE html>
<html>
```

```html
<head>
    <meta charset="UTF-8">
    <meta name="viewport" content="width=device-width, initial-scale=1.0">
    <title>Play Music File</title>
    <link rel="stylesheet" href="panner.css">
</head>

<body>
    <input type="file" name="music" id="filePicker" accept="audio/*">
    <script>
      var audioCtx = new AudioContext();
      var bufferSource = audioCtx.createBufferSource();
      bufferSource.connect(audioCtx.destination); //bufferSource-->destination

      function playMusic(evt) {
        const musicBuffer = evt.target.result; //Get undecoded audio data
        audioCtx.decodeAudioData(musicBuffer).then((decodeAudio) => {
          bufferSource.buffer = decodeAudio; //Decoded audio data
          bufferSource.loop = true;
          bufferSource.start(); //start playing
        }).catch((error) => console.log(error));
      }

      function readFile(evt) {
        var reader = new FileReader();
        reader.addEventListener("load", playMusic); //Call the playMusic() function when the file is read
          reader.readAsArrayBuffer(evt.target.files[0]);
      }
      window.addEventListener("load", () => {
        document.getElementById("filePicker").addEventListener("change", readFile);
      });
    </script>
</body>

</html>
```

When we select a music file through the <input> element, call the readFile(evt) function. This function successfully reads the music file and then calls the playMusic(evt) function, and then calls decodeAudioData() to decode the undecoded audio stored in the musicBuffer, finally call the start() method to play after successful decoding.

Let's add a volume control node based on this example.

4.5 Control Volume

The GainNode node is used to control the volume, which is created by the AudioContext.createGain() method. GainNode has only one input port and one output port, the number of channels is 2, the upmix/downmix strategy is "speaker", and the channel count mode is "max". In addition to inheriting the properties and methods of the AudioNode object, it adds a gain property of the AudioParam interface type to change the volume-setting gain.value or calling the method of the AudioParam interface. Refer to Figure 4.13.

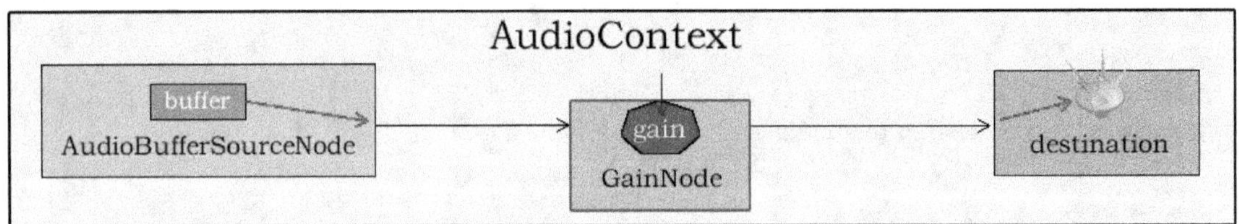

Figure 4.13 GainNode node usage example

The properties and methods of the AudioParam interface are introduced as follows:

defaultValue - Read-only attribute, which represents the default volume at the beginning.

value - Writable attribute, representing the current volume. The initial value is equal to defaultValue.

maxValue/minValue - Read-only attributes, which define the value range of the *value* attribute.

setValueAtTime(newValue, startTime) - Change the value of the attribute *value* to *newValue* at the specified time *startTime*. The parameter *startTime* is a double-precision type, which defines the number of seconds since the creation of the AudioContext, usually in the form of AudioContext.currentTime+n, where AudioContext.currentTime represents the number of seconds since the creation of the AudioContext to the present. For example, setValueAtTime(0.5, AudioContext.currentTime+5) means that the volume is adjusted to half of the maximum volume after 5 seconds.

linearRampToValueAtTime(newValue, endTime) - from now to endTime, linearly adjust the value of the attribute vlue to newValue, so that the fade in and fade out sound effect can be achieved for the GainNode node. For example, linearRampToValueAtTime(0, AudioContext.currentTime+2) fades out the sound within 2 seconds.

exponentialRampToValueAtTime(newValue, endTime) - Change the volume according to the exponential curve. It usually used to adjust the audio frequency or playback rate.

setTargetAtTime(newValue, startTime, timeConstant) - Adjust the value of the attribute *value* to *newValue* according to the exponential curve after *timeConstant* seconds from *startTime*. E.g: gainNode.gain.setTargetAtTime(0, audioCtx.currentTime + 1, 1.5).

setValueCurveAtTime(values, startTime, duration) – The value of the attribute *value* is changed according to the polyline formed by the vertex coordinates $\left(values[i], startTime + \left(\dfrac{duration}{values.length - 1} \right) \times i \right)$ defined by the floating-point array *values* within duration seconds from the *startTime* time. E.g:

setValueCurveAtTime([0.5, 1, 0.5, 0, 0.5, 1, 0.5, 0, 0.5], audioCtx.currentTime + 1, 4);

The drawn coordinates are shown in Figure 4.14, and the value of the attribute *value* changes according to the polyline in the coordinates.

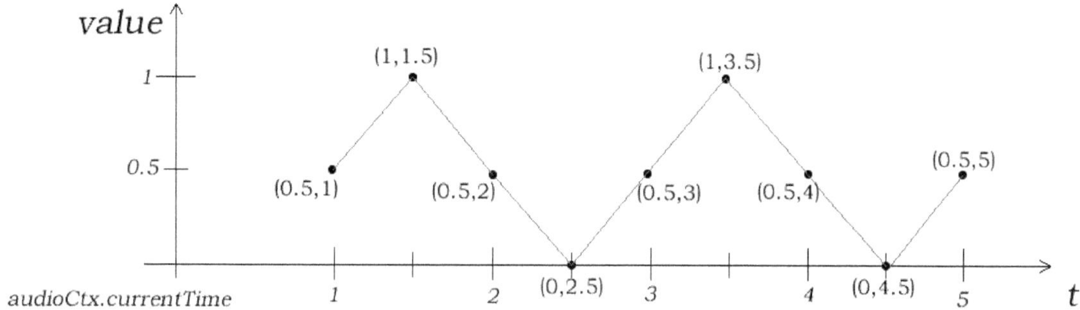

Figure 4.14 Change the volume according to the broken line

cancelScheduledValues(startTime) – Cancel all tasks that are taking effect or will take effect after the *startTime*, except for tasks that are in effect when this method is called. The tasks scheduled after this method is called continue to be effective. For example, cancelScheduledValues(audioCtx.currentTime) cancels all tasks, but the tasks currently in effect are not affected.

cancelAndHoldAtTime(startTime) - Cancel all tasks that will take effect after the *startTime*, and the tasks that are in effect at the *startTime* are terminated immediately, but the value of the attribute *value* is retained. Look at the example:

```
gain.value = 1;
gain.linearRampToValueAtTime(3, audioContext.currentTime + 2);
gain.cancelAndHoldAtTime(audioContext.currentTime + 1);
//gain.cancelScheduledValues(audioContext.currentTime + 1);
```

The current value of attribute *value* is 1 (the first statement), and within 2 seconds from now, the value of *value* will linearly become 3 (the second statement), and the task in effect will be cancelled at 1 second (ie, the second statement defined task), but at this time the value of *value* has changed to 2, so its value continues to maintain 2. But if the third sentence is changed to the fourth sentence that is annotated, then the task arranged by the second sentence will not start at all, so the value of the attribute *value* is unchanged, it is still 1.

We add two buttons to the example in the previous section. When we click the buttons, the sound gradually fades out or fades in, and then add <input> element with range type to control the volume.

```
<input type="file" name="music" id="filePicker" accept="audio/*">
<input id="volume" type="range" min="0" max="100" value="100">
<span>control volume</span>
<button id="fakeout">Fade Out</button> <button id="fakein">Fade In</button>
<script>
  var audioCtx = new AudioContext();
  var bufferSource = audioCtx.createBufferSource();
  var gainNode = audioCtx.createGain();
  bufferSource.connect(gainNode).connect(audioCtx.destination); //bufferSource-->gainNode-->destination

  function gainVolume(evt) {
    gainNode.gain.value = parseFloat(evt.target.value / 100.0);
  }
  function fakeoutVolume(evt) {
    gainNode.gain.linearRampToValueAtTime(0.0,audioCtx.currentTime + 2);
  }
  function fakeinVolume(evt) {
    gainNode.gain.setTargetAtTime(1.0, audioCtx.currentTime, 3);
  }
  document.getElementById("volume").addEventListener("change",gainVolume);
  document.getElementById("fakeout").addEventListener("click", fakeoutVolume);
  document.getElementById("fakein").addEventListener("click", fakeinVolume);

  function playMusic(evt) {
```

Codes other than gray are newly added. Drag the slider to adjust the volume, click the "Fade Out" button, and the sound will gradually decrease until silent. On the contrary, click the "Fade In" button, and the sound will gradually increase from silent. The browsing effect is shown in Figure 4.15.

Figure 4.15 Add volume control

4.6 Split/Merge Channel

We split the channels on the basis of the subsection "§4.5 Controlling the Volume", and delay processing one of the channels, and finally merge the channels and play again. The audio processing directed diagram is shown in Figure 4.16.

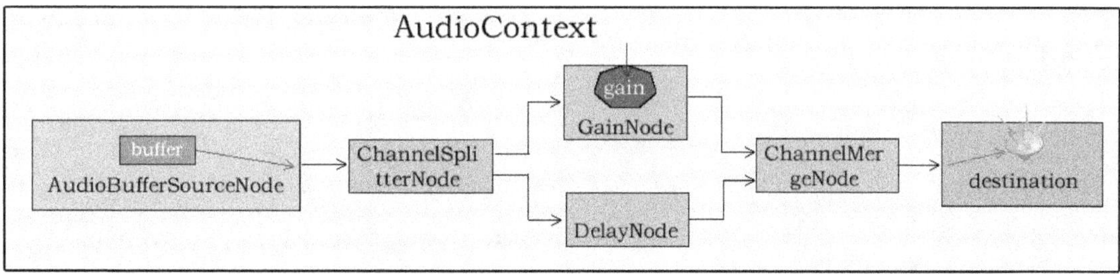

Figure 4.16 Add channel split node

The ChannelSplitterNode node is relatively simple. It can be instantiated directly with AudioContext.createChannelSplitter(numberOfOutputs), where numberOfOutput specifies the number of channels after splitting, and one channel occupies one output port. Similarly, the channel merge node ChannelMergerNode is instantiated using AudioContext.createChannelMerger(numberOfInputs). The delay node DelayNode is instantiated by AudioContext.createDelay(maxDelayTime), where the parameter maxDelayTime defines the maximum delay in seconds, the value range is [1,180], and the default is 1 second. The specific delay in seconds should be set to the AudioParam interface type. Property delayTime (see the gain property of gainNode for the method). On the basis of the previous example, add the following code except gray.

```javascript
var audioCtx = new AudioContext();
var bufferSource = audioCtx.createBufferSource();
var gainNode = audioCtx.createGain();
var spliterNode = audioCtx.createChannelSplitter(2);
var mergerNode = audioCtx.createChannelMerger(2);
var delayNode = audioCtx.createDelay(10.0);
delayNode.delayTime.setValueAtTime(2.0, audioCtx.currentTime);

bufferSource.connect(spliterNode);//bufferSource-->spliterNode
spliterNode.connect(gainNode,1);
spliterNode.connect(delayNode,0);
gainNode.connect(mergerNode,0,0);
delayNode.connect(mergerNode,0,1);
mergerNode.connect(audioCtx.destination);

function gainVolume(evt){
    gainNode.gain.value = parseFloat(evt.target.value/100.0);
}
```

4.7 Audio Visualization

Graphically display the audio volume or the amplitude of each frequency. At this time, the AnalyserNode node is used, which uses fast Fourier transform (FFT) to split the audio into sine waves of several frequencies, and then just visualize them, or visualize the sampled data used by FFT directly. The most commonly used method for drawing real-time animation graphics is to use the <canvas> element and requestAnimationFrame() method. We add AnalyserNode to the bypass in front of the destination node, as shown in Figure 4.17.

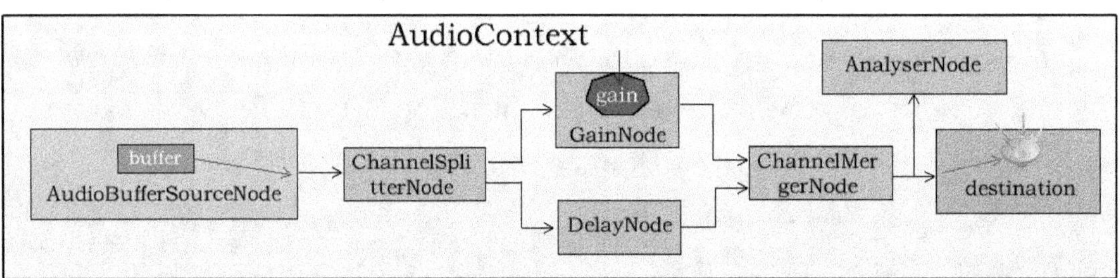

Figure 4.17 Add audio visualization node

The attributes and methods of the AnalyserNode node are introduced as follows:

fftsize - The number of sample data used for each execution of the Fast Fourier Transform. The value is generally a power of 2, and the default is 2048.

frequencyBinCount - A read-only attribute that stores the number of sine waves of different frequencies that are split, which is equal to one-half of the *fftsize*.

minDecibels/maxDecibels – Define the minimum and maximum decibels respectively. After the audio is split into sine waves of different frequencies, the amplitude of the sine wave with an amplitude equal to or less than minDecibels is set to 0.0 (when getFloatFrequencyData() obtains frequency domain data) or 0 (when getByteFrequencyData() obtains frequency domain data), The amplitude of a sine wave equal to or greater than maxDecibels is set to 1.0 or 255. Since the amplitudes of sine waves of different frequencies calculated by the FFT are all negative numbers, the minDecibels and maxDecibels values are 0 or negative, and 0 represents the largest sound. If we use the getByteFrequencyData() method to obtain frequency domain data, the interval [minDecibels,maxDecibels] is mapped to the interval [0,255], so the amplitude Y_k of the sine wave with frequency k is converted to

$$\left| \frac{255}{maxDecibels - minDecibels} \times (Y_k - minDecibels) \right|$$

on the interval [0,255]. The default value of minDecibels is -100, and the default value of maxDecibels is -30.

smoothingTimeConstant – The smoothing constant of time series data defines the degree of correlation between two values that have a sequential relationship in time. 0 means no correlation, 1 means two values are heavily correlated (almost equal), and the default is 0.8. For example, the amplitude of a sine wave with frequency k was calculated as Y1 last time, and the value calculated this time is Y2. If the smoothing constant is set to 0, then Y2 is directly output this time, otherwise, their associated values are calculated and output (between Y1 and Y2), so the drawn curve is smoother.

getFloatFrequencyData(dataArray) – Copy the frequency spectrum data calculated by FFT to the dataArray array of Float32Array type. The number of elements in the dataArray array is generally equal to AnalyserNode.frequencyBinCount. If they are not equal, the extra ones are ignored. The spectrum value corresponding to mute is -Infinity. datArray[i] is the amplitude (decibel) of the sine wave with frequency i. Generally, the smaller the frequency, the larger the amplitude.

getByteFrequencyData(dataArray) - Copy the spectrum data calculated by FFT to the dataArray array of Uint8Array type, and the decibel value is mapped to the interval [0,255]. If high precision is required, please use the getFloatFrequencyData() method.

getFloatTimeDomainData(dataArray) – Directly copy the sampled data (time domain data) involved in the FFT calculation to the dataArray array of Float32Array type. The number of elements in the dataArray array is generally equal to AnalyserNode.fftsize. datArray[i] is the data of the i+1th sample. The number of time domain data is twice that of frequency domain data.

getByteTimeDomainData(dataArray) - Directly copy the sampled data (time domain data) involved in the FFT calculation to the dataArray array of Uint8Array type.

The code in this section is as follows:

```html
<body>
<canvas id="visualizer" height="120px" width="800px"></canvas><br>
    //The statement here refers to the code in the previous section
  mergerNode.connect(audioCtx.destination);

  const canvas = document.getElementById("visualizer");
  const analyser = audioCtx.createAnalyser();
  mergerNode.connect(analyser);
  visualize();
  function visualize() {
    const canvasCtx = canvas.getContext("2d");
    //The analyser.fftsize defaults to 2048, so every time you do FFT calculation, 2048 is used for the sampled
data to generate 1024 sine waves of different frequencies
    const bufferLength = analyser.frequencyBinCount; //1024
    const dataArray = new Uint8Array(bufferLength);

    var linear = canvasCtx.createLinearGradient(0, 0, 0,canvas.height);
    linear.addColorStop(0, "red");
    linear.addColorStop(0.7, "blue");
    linear.addColorStop(1, "green");

    draw()
```

```javascript
function draw() {
    const hWIDTH = canvas.width / 2;
    const HEIGHT = canvas.height;

    analyser.getByteFrequencyData(dataArray);
    canvasCtx.fillStyle = 'rgb(200, 200, 200)';
    canvasCtx.lineWidth = 2;
    canvasCtx.strokeStyle = linear;
    canvasCtx.fillRect(0, 0, canvas.width, HEIGHT);

    canvasCtx.beginPath();

    let step = Math.floor(bufferLength * 3.0 / hWIDTH);
    let x = 0;

    for (let i = 0; i < bufferLength; i = i + step) {
        let y = dataArray[i] * HEIGHT / 256;
        canvasCtx.moveTo(hWIDTH + x, HEIGHT);
        canvasCtx.lineTo(hWIDTH + x, HEIGHT - y);
        canvasCtx.moveTo(hWIDTH - x, HEIGHT);
        canvasCtx.lineTo(hWIDTH - x, HEIGHT - y);
        x += 3;
    }
    canvasCtx.stroke();
    requestAnimationFrame(draw);
    }
}

function gainVolume(evt) {
    gainNode.gain.value = parseFloat(evt.target.value / 100.0);
}
```

The browsing effect is shown in Figure 4.18.

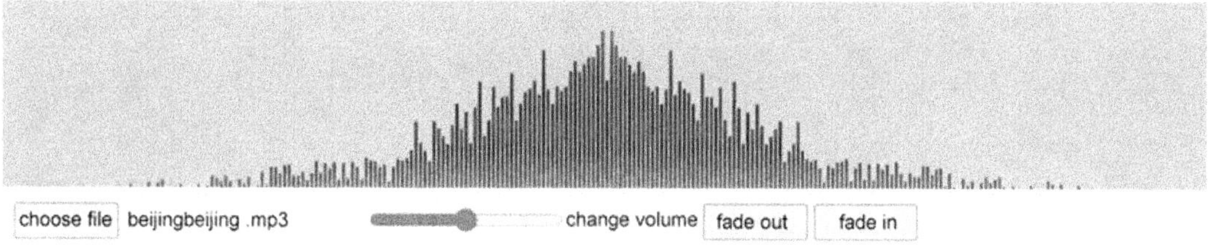

Figure 4.18 Audio visualization example

Let's try to modify analyzer.minDecibels = -120, analyzer.maxDecibels = -1, analyzer.smoothingTimeConstant = 0.6, and think how it works?

We continue to add audio filters based on the previous example to filter some high-frequency or low-frequency signals. Both IIRFilterNode and BiquadFilterNode nodes can achieve filtering, but the former is a general filter, while the latter is a special case of the former, so the latter can be used directly to quickly achieve filtering that meets some specific occasions, but if the former is used, the filter can be defined more flexibly Parameters to customize the most suitable filter for various occasions. The BiquadFilterNode node can implement several types of filters, tone controllers, and equalizers. This time we add the BiquadFilterNode node after the ChannelMergerNode node, see Figure 4.19.

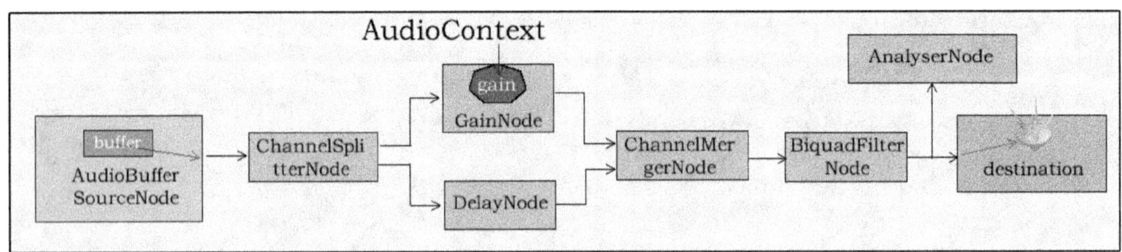

Figure 4.19 Add audio filter node

You can use AudioContxt.createBiquadFilter() to instantiate a BiquadFilterNode node. Its properties and methods are described as follows:

frequency - Its type is AudioParam. This attribute defines the reference frequency (unit: Hz) in the current algorithm, the default value is 350Hz. For example, frquency.value=5000, if it is high-pass filtering, the signal below 5000Hz will be filtered out, if it is low-pass filtering, the signal above 5000Hz will be filtered out.

detune – The frequency is changed in unit of cent, 100 cents equals one semitone. The type of this attribute is AudioParam, and the default value is 0. For example, detune.value = 100 means to increase a semitone, and detune.value=-200 means to decrease a whole tone.

Q – This is a dimensionless quality factor of AudioParam type. The default value is 1, and the value range is generally [0.0001,1000]. It is defined as the ratio of the peak energy stored in the resonator during an oscillation cycle to the energy lost per radian in that cycle. The higher the Q value, the weaker the damping, and the longer the oscillation time without increasing energy. For example, the same pendulum has a higher Q value when it oscillates in the air, but a lower Q value when it is immersed in oil. Refer to Figure 4.20.

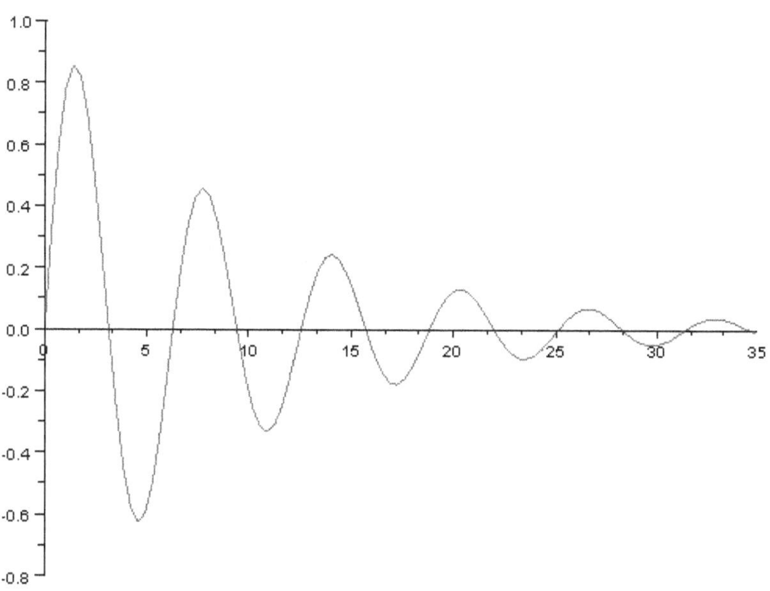

A small Q value means that the oscillation stops quickly

Figure 4.20 The larger the Q value, the smaller the damping

gain - Indicates the gain (amplified or attenuated volume) used in the current filtering algorithm. It is of type AudioParam, the unit is dB, and the default value is 0. When it takes a positive value, it is a real gain, and when it takes a negative value, it is an attenuation. The value range is -40 to 40. It is different from gainNode, gainNode is adjusted between mute and maximum volume (assuming maxVolume), and this gain attribute is adjusted between [maxVolume-40, maxVolume+40].

type – Define the algorithm executed by the BiquadFilterNode node. Different algorithms have different functions. The default is "lowpass", which is a low-pass filter. The value of the type attribute is an enumerated type, and the combination with other attributes is shown in Table 4.3.

Table 4.3 Filtering algorithm

type	Description	frequency	Q	gain
lowpass	Standard second-order resonant low-pass filter with 12dB/octave attenuation. The frequencies	Cut-off frequency	Define the degree of attenuation of	No effect

	below the cutoff frequency pass, and the frequencies above it are attenuated.		frequencies near the cutoff frequency. The larger the Q value, the smaller the attenuation.	
highpass	Standard second-order resonant high-pass filter with 12dB/octave attenuation. Frequencies below the cutoff frequency are attenuated; frequencies above it pass.	Cut-off frequency	Define the degree of attenuation of frequencies near the cutoff frequency. The larger the Q value, the smaller the attenuation.	No effect
bandpass	Standard second-order band pass filter. The frequencies outside the given frequency range will be attenuated, and the frequencies within the range will pass.	Center frequency within a given range	Control the width of the frequency band. The larger the Q value, the larger the frequency band.	No effect
notch	Standard notch filter, also called band stop or band stop filter. Contrary to the band pass filter: the frequency beyond the given frequency range is passed, and the internal frequency is attenuated.	Center frequency within a given range	Control the width of the frequency band. The larger the Q value, the larger the frequency band.	No effect
lowshelf	Standard second-order lowshell filter, allowing all frequencies to pass, but frequencies lower than the reference frequency will be enhanced or attenuated	Reference frequency	No effect	A positive number means gain, and a negative number means attenuation.
highshelf	Standard second-order hightshell filter, allowing all frequencies to pass, but frequencies higher than the reference frequency will be gain or attenuated	Reference frequency	No effect	A positive number means gain, and a negative number means attenuation.
peaking	The peak filter allows all frequencies to pass, but the frequencies within a given range will be gain or attenuated, and the frequencies outside the range remain unchanged	Center frequency within a given range	Control the width of the frequency band. The larger the Q value, the larger the frequency band.	A positive number means gain, and a negative number means attenuation.
allpass	Standard second-order all-pass filter. It allows all frequencies to pass, but it changes the phase relationship between the	The center frequency at which the phase	Defines the sharpness of the phase transition at the center	No effect

	frequencies.	change occurs.	frequency, the larger the Q value, the steeper the transition and the greater the group delay	

Add the following code to the example in the previous section:

```
delayNode.connect(mergerNode, 0, 1);
var filterNode = audioCtx.createBiquadFilter();
//filterNode.frequency.value = 250;
mergerNode.connect(filterNode).connect(audioCtx.destination);

const canvas = document.getElementById("visualizer");
const analyser = audioCtx.createAnalyser();
filterNode.connect(analyser);
visualize();
```

All properties of the filter take the default values, namely the reference frequency 350Hz, Q value 1 (rapidly attenuated), and low-pass filter. The resulting sound effect is that audio frequencies higher than 350Hz are filtered out (rapidly attenuated). By observing the visual graph, we found that there is only a bar in the middle. Make the commented statement of the above code take effect, and then take a look at how the visualization changes. You can also use the following statement to gradually modify the value of frequency:

```
filterNode.frequency.exponentialRampToValueAtTime(10, audioCtx.currentTime + 30);
```

The following statement implements a lowshelf filter with audio with a gain lower than the reference frequency:

```
filterNode.type = "lowshelf";
filterNode.gain.value = 20;
mergerNode.connect(filterNode).connect(audioCtx.destination);
```

4.9 Convolution

You should have heard the song "Eighteen Bends on the Mountain Road". Li Qiong sang in front of the valley by the stream halfway up the mountain. The singing reverberated in the valley for a long time, making people fascinated. But I want to tell you that she recorded the song in a quiet recording studio, and then convolved it with the impulse response audio (Impulse Rsponse, or IR) recorded in the valley. You may not believe it. The ConvolverNode node introduced in this section completes the convolution reverberation function. In the past, a hardware convolution reverberation device was very expensive, and even now, it is not cheap!

Convolutional reverberation involves two pieces of audio: one is dry sound-audio that is processed by convolution, such as "Eighteen Bends on the Mountain Road" recorded by Li Qiong in a quiet recording studio, and the other is recorded in the sound space, it is short (usually less than 5 seconds) impulse response audio, such as setting off a firecracker or firing a shot in a valley, record the gunfire and subsequent echoes, and save it in wav format. There are several requirements for recording impulse response audio: (1) Recording in sound spaces with reverberation reflections, such as auditoriums, valleys, tunnels, etc., reverberation reflections are the response to the original sound. (2)The original sound should be completed as soon as possible (an impact on the surrounding environment) , And the sound frequency range is as wide as possible, that is, it contains as many frequencies as possible, such as firing a shot. (3) Store in a lossless format, such as wav format. (4) Terminate the recording in time after the response sound of the original sound disappears, or cut the head and tail when doing post-processing, we must ensure that the impulse response audio is effective and short-lived (disappears within a few seconds), and the original sound and the impulse response audio have the same sampling rate. There are many impulse response audio materials for selection on the Internet. These materials are found in various sound environments. If the same sing you record is convolved and reverberated with the impulse response audio of the auditorium, the effect will be the same as if you were standing in the auditorium singing. The impact response audio convolution reverberation, the effect is the same as you are standing in a valley singing.

The execution process of convolution reverberation is roughly like this: First, the two audio segments are split into sine waves of various frequencies through Fourier transform, and then for each sine wave of the audio to be processed, the impulse response of the same frequency is found. The output sine wave (so the wider the sound range, the better), the two sine waves are multiplied and accumulated like this: assuming that at the time point *n*, the sample of the two sine waves are set to *f(n)* and *g(n)*, respectively. After the product reverberation is set to *v(n)*, then there is a formula:

$$v(n) = \sum_{t=0}^{n} (f(t) \times g(n-t))$$

g(n-t) is the result of scrolling *g(t)* from left to right, and then multiplied by *f(t)*, and finally accumulated. To describe in plain language is: according to the reverberation data of the impulse response audio, do the same reverberation processing for the dry sound.

Next, we use the ConvolverNode node to complete the convolution. First, sing a song by ourselves and record it. After decoding, put it into the buffer of AudioBufferSourceNode as the convolved dry sound. Then download an impulse response audio from the Internet, and place it in the convolverNode.buffer after decoding. The audio processing directed graph is shown in Figure 4.21.

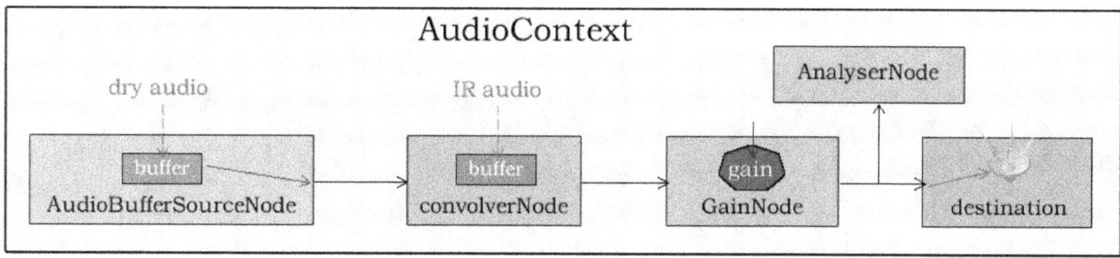

Figure 4.21 The processing directed graph with convolverNode

You can use AudioContext.crteateConvolver() to instantiate the convolverNode node, which performs linear convolution on the original stem on the decoded audio stored in its buffer attribute. The convolverNode object has two properties:

buffer – It is audioBuffer interface type, used to store mono, dual, or four-channel impulse response decoded audio.

normalize – It is a Boolean type, which controls whether to scale the impulse response audio data by the idempotent normalization method when setting the buffer attribute. The default is true, that is, the output of the convolver is more uniform after idempotent normalization. Note: If the value of this attribute is modified, it will take effect only when the buffer attribute is modified next time.

Next, I give a complete example. First, prepare two audio files on the local disk, one is a normal music file, in any format, and the other is an impulse response audio. The browsing effect is shown in Figure 4.22.

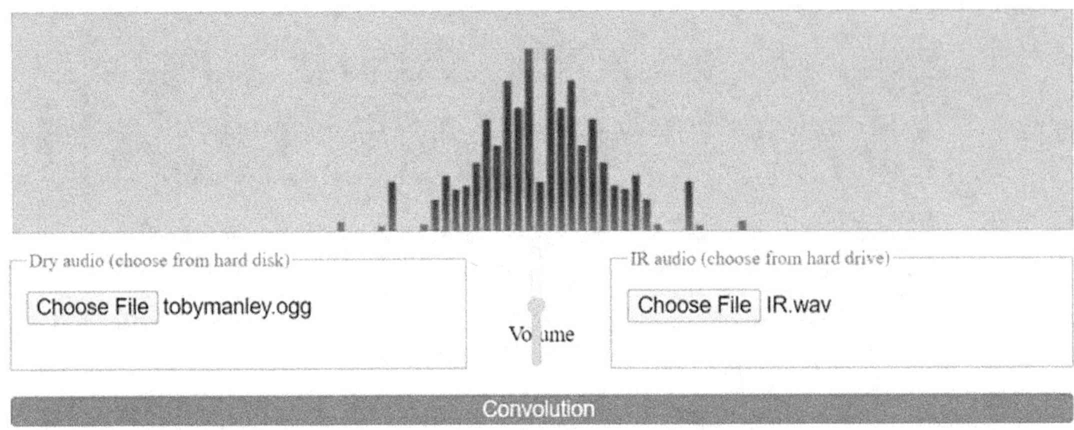

Figure 4.22 Audio convolution processing example

The complete code is as follows:

```html
<!DOCTYPE html>
<html>

<head>
    <meta charset="UTF-8">
    <meta name="viewport" content="width=device-width, initial-scale=1.0">
    <title>AudioContext- convolution</title>
    <style>
        * {
            margin: 0px;
            font-size: 18px;
        }

        #out-container {
            width: 900px;
            margin: 10px auto;
        }

        #canvas {
            width: 100%;
            height: 180px;
            border: 1px solid grey;
            margin-bottom: 20px;
        }

        #in-container {
```

```css
            display: flex;
            justify-content: space-between;
            width: 100%;
            height: 100px;
        }

        fieldset {
            width: 360px;
            height: 80%;
            border: 1px solid grey;
        }

        #vol-box {
            height: 100%;
            width: 50px;
            position: relative;
            margin-top: 40px;
        }

        input[type="file"] {
            margin-top: 10px;
        }

        #volume {
            transform: rotate(-90deg) translateY(-27px);
            width: 100px;
        }

        legend {
            font-size: 16px;
            color: #666;
        }

        #convolve {
            margin: 20px 0px;
            background-color: #009726;
            display: block;
            width: 100%;
            color: white;
            border: 1px solid grey;
            border-radius: 4px;
        }
    </style>
</head>

<body>
    <div id="out-container">
        <canvas id="canvas">Your browser does not support the &lt;canvas&gt; element</canvas>
        <section id="in-container">
            <fieldset>
                <legend>Dry audio (choose from hard disk)</legend>
                <input type="file" id="music-file" accept="audio/*">
```

```html
            </fieldset>
            <div id="vol-box">
                <input id="volume" type="range" min="0" max="100" value="50" disabled><br>
                <span>Volume</span>
            </div>
            <fieldset>
                <legend>IR audio (choose from hard drive)</legend>
                <input type="file" id="ir-file" accept="audio/wav">
            </fieldset>
        </section>
        <button id="convolve">Convolution</button>
    </div>
    <script>
        var audioCtx, bufferSource, convolver, gain, analyser;
        var musicFile, irFile, convole;

        window.addEventListener("load", () => {
            document.getElementById("volume").addEventListener("change", gainVolume);
            convolve = document.getElementById("convolve");
            convolve.addEventListener("click", convolveStart);

            audioCtx = new (window.AudioContext || window.webkitAudioContext)();
            bufferSource = audioCtx.createBufferSource();
            convolver = audioCtx.createConvolver();
            gain = audioCtx.createGain();
            analyser = audioCtx.createAnalyser();

            bufferSource.connect(convolver).connect(gain).connect(audioCtx.destination);
            gain.connect(analyser);
            musicFile = document.getElementById("music-file");
            irFile = document.getElementById("ir-file");
        });

        function convolveStart() {
            if (musicFile.files.length < 1 || irFile.files.length < 1) {
                alert("Please select an audio file from the hard disk first!");
                return;
            }
            convolve.textContent = "Convolving ...";
            convolve.disbled = true;

            let reader = new FileReader();
            reader.addEventListener("load", musicFinished);
            reader.readAsArrayBuffer(musicFile.files[0]);

        }

        async function musicFinished(evt) {
            let musicBuffer1 = evt.target.result;
            bufferSource.loop = true;
            bufferSource.buffer = await audioCtx.decodeAudioData(musicBuffer1);
```

```javascript
    let reader = new FileReader();
    reader.addEventListener("load", irFinished);
    reader.readAsArrayBuffer(irFile.files[0]);
}

async function irFinished(evt) {
    let musicBuffer2 = evt.target.result;
    convolver.buffer = await audioCtx.decodeAudioData(musicBuffer2);
    bufferSource.start();
    visualize();
    convolve.textContent = "Convolution";
    convolve.disbled = false;
    document.getElementById("volume").disabled = false;
}

function gainVolume(evt) {
    gain.gain.value = parseFloat(evt.target.value / 100.0);
}

function visualize() {
    let canvas = document.getElementById("canvas");
    const canvasCtx = canvas.getContext("2d");
    const bufferLength = analyser.frequencyBinCount;
    const dataArray = new Uint8Array(bufferLength);

    var linear = canvasCtx.createLinearGradient(0, 0, 0, canvas.height);
    linear.addColorStop(0, "red");
    linear.addColorStop(0.7, "blue");
    linear.addColorStop(1, "green");

    draw()

    function draw() {
        const hWIDTH = canvas.width / 2;
        const HEIGHT = canvas.height;

        analyser.getByteFrequencyData(dataArray);
        canvasCtx.fillStyle = 'rgb(200, 200, 200)';
        canvasCtx.lineWidth = 2;
        canvasCtx.strokeStyle = linear;
        canvasCtx.fillRect(0, 0, canvas.width, HEIGHT);

        canvasCtx.beginPath();

        let step = Math.floor(bufferLength * 3.0 / hWIDTH);
        let x = 0;

        for (let i = 0; i < bufferLength; i = i + step) {
            let y = dataArray[i] * HEIGHT / 256;
            canvasCtx.moveTo(hWIDTH + x, HEIGHT);
            canvasCtx.lineTo(hWIDTH + x, HEIGHT - y);
            canvasCtx.moveTo(hWIDTH - x, HEIGHT);
```

```
                canvasCtx.lineTo(hWIDTH - x, HEIGHT - y);
                x += 3;
            }
            canvasCtx.stroke();
            requestAnimationFrame(draw);
        }
    }
    </script>
</body>

</html>
```

4.10 3D Surround

3D surround involves the position of the listener and the position of the sound source, and the listener also involves the two parameters: one is the angle between the horizontal line and the line through both ears, and the other is the listener's face orientation. The sound source also involves the two parameters of the orientation and the angle of the sound cone. The 3D space of the computer conforms to the right-handed coordinate system, see diagram 4.23 for details.

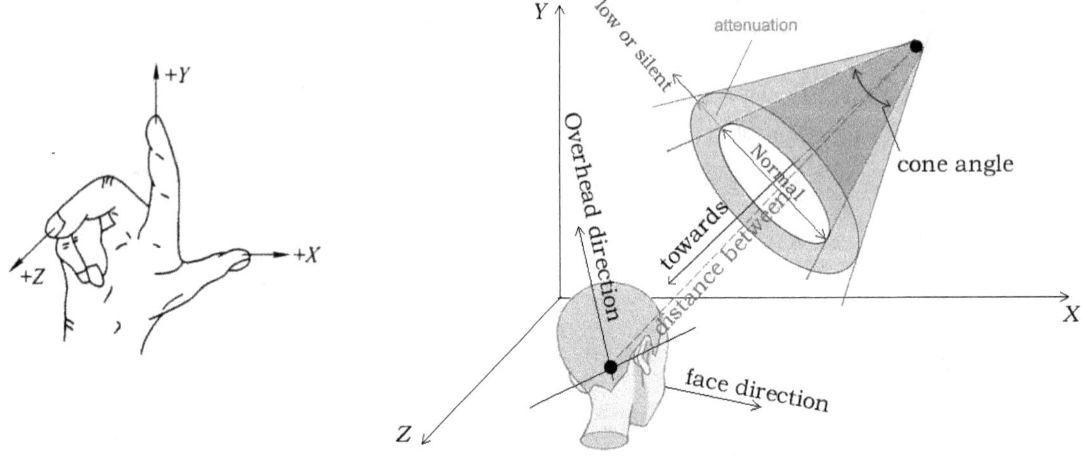

Figure 4.23 Listener and sound source in 3D environment

The face orientation of the listener is the direction of the tip of the human nose. The orientation of the top of the head, the face orientation, and the connection line between the two ears are perpendicular to each other, so we indirectly determine the direction line of the two ears by determining the orientation of the top of the head and the face orientation. The central ray of the sound cone is the direction of the sound source. Inside the sound cone is the normal volume, and there is a gradually attenuating cone outside the sound cone, and then there is silent or very small sound outside. The Z coordinate is perpendicular to the screen and pointing to the human eye.

Use the PannerNode node to define the sound source in the 3D space, including three parameters: position, orientation, and cone angle, and use the attribute listener of AudioContext to define the listener in the 3D space, including three parameters: position, face, and head direction.

The PannerNode node has an input port and an output port. The input port allows mono or dual channels, while the output port has only dual channels. Use AudioContext.createPanner() to instantiate a PannerNode object. The properties and methods of this object are described as follows:

coneInnerAngle - It is a double-precision type. It defines the angle of the cone. The unit is degree. The default is 360 degrees (the sound has no direction). The sound will not decay in the cone. e.g.: panner.coneInnerAngle=30.

coneOuterAngle - Double-precision type, defines the angle of the cone that the volume is gradually attenuated, the unit is degrees, the default is 0 degrees, the outer volume of the gradually attenuating cone is very small or silent (specifically defined by the coneOuterGain attribute). From the sound cone to the volume attenuation cone, the sound gradually becomes smaller, that is, the normal volume transitions to the volume defined by the coneOuterGain attribute. Such as panner.coneOuterAngle=46

coneOuterGain – Double-precision type, defines the volume level outside the attenuation cone, the value range is [0,1], and the default is 0 (ie silent).

maxDistance – It is a double-precision non-negative number type. It defines the maximum distance between the sound source and the listener. When the distance is greater than this, the volume will not change. The default value is 10000.

refDistance - It is a double-precision non-negative number type and defines the reference distance. When the distance between the sound source and the listener is greater than this distance, the volume starts to attenuate, and the default value is 1. Generally, maxDistance is greater than refDistance.

distanceModel – The algorithm that defines the volume attenuation when the sound source is far away from the listener can be as follows:

(1) "linear": linear attenuation, the attenuation formula is 1-rolloffFactor * (distance-refDistance) / (maxDistance-refDistance), where distance is the current distance between the listener and the sound source.

(2)"inverse" (default): The volume attenuation formula is

$$refDistnce \div (refDistance + rolloffFctor \times (max(distance, refDistance) - refDistance)).$$

(3) "exponential": Volume exponential attenuation, the attenuation formula is

$$\left(\frac{refDistance}{max(distnce, refDistance)}\right)^{rolloffFactor}.$$

rolloffFactor – When the sound source moves from the reference distance (defined by the refDistance attribute) to the maximum distance (defined by the maxDistance attribute), define the attenuation volume, the default value is 1. The value range is related to the distanceModel attribute: (1)When distanceModel="linear", the value range is [0,1]; (2)When distanceModel="inverse" or "exponential", the value range is $[0, +\infty]$.

Refer to Figure 4.24 for the relationship between the above attributes.

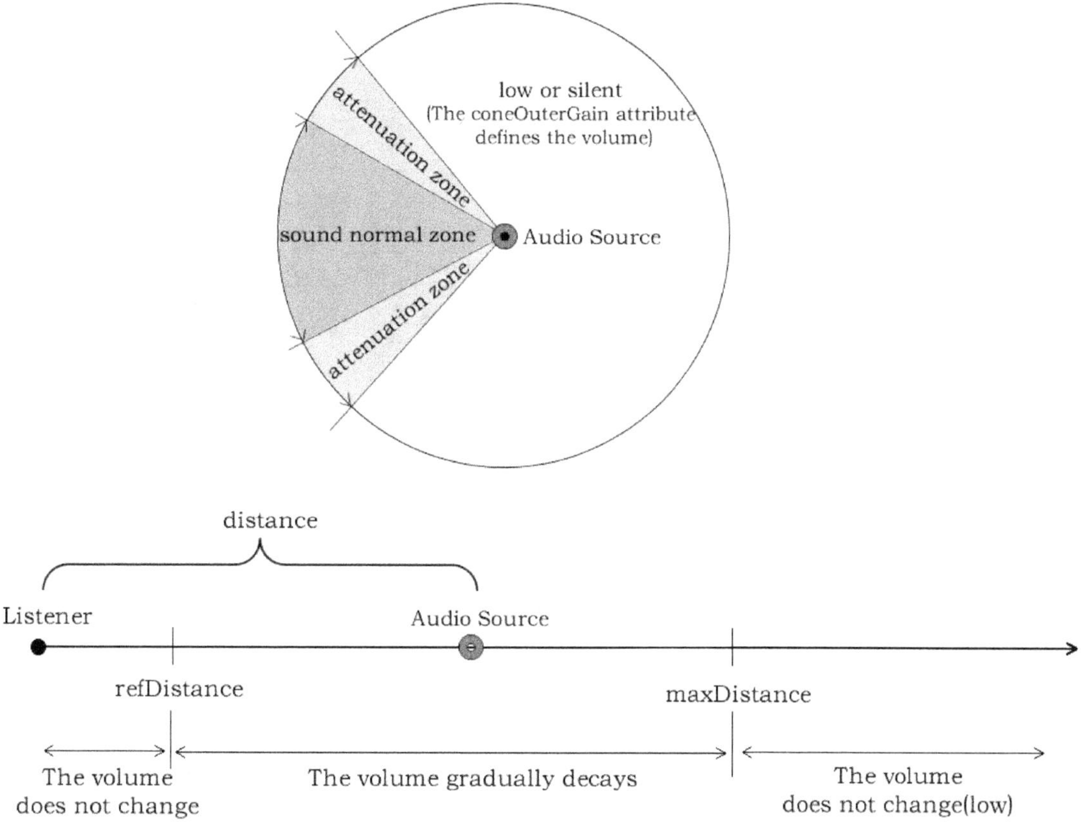

Figure 4.24 The distance and angle between the listener and the sound source

orientation/orientation/orientationZ – Their type are AudioParam, which define the vector of the audio source orientation, that is, point from (0,0,0) to (orientationX, orientationY, orientationZ), and the default value is (1,0,0), which is the X axis direction. For example, orientationY.value=5 changes the value of the Y coordinate to 5. This assignment statement is equivalent to orientationY.setValueAtTime(5, audioCtx.currentTime).

position/positionY/positionZ – All are AudioParam interface types, which define the position coordinates of the audio source. The default value is (0,0,0), which is at the origin of the coordinate system.

panningModel - Determine the algorithm for positioning the audio in the 3D space. The values can be "equalpower" (simple and effective equal power translation algorithm. This is the default value), "HRTF" (convolution reverberation into stereo output, the sense of space is better than the equalpower algorithm, but it also consumes more computing resources). The schematic diagram is shown in Figure 4.25.

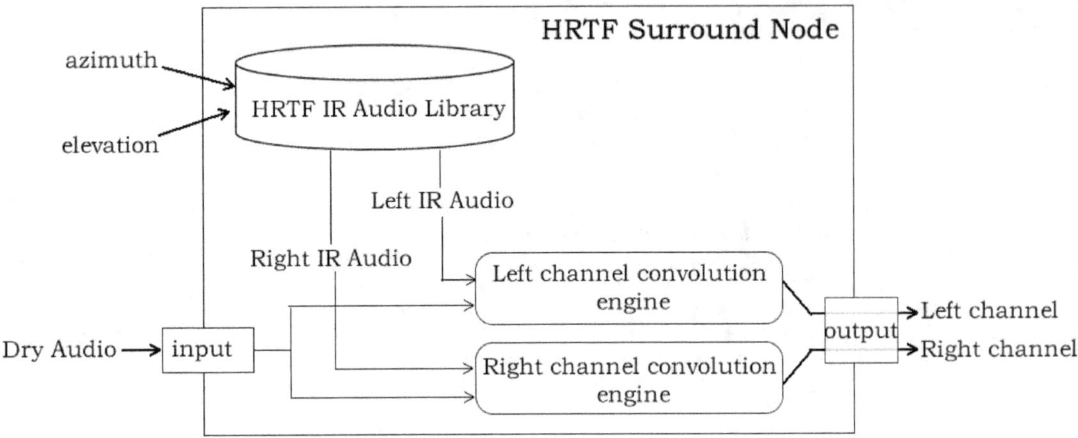

Figure 4.25 PanningModel attribute description

setPosition([x, y, z]) – Set the position coordinates of the sound source, that is, set the value of the positionX, positionY, and positionZ properties. If the function parameters are omitted, it is set at the origin of the coordinates, that is (0,0,0).

setOrientation([x, y, z]) – Set the orientation of the sound source, that is, set the values of orientationX, orientationY, and orientationZ properties. If the function parameters are omitted, set it to (1,0,0), which is the direction of the X axis.

Use AudioContext.listener property to determine the relevant information of the listener, that is, position, face and head direction. This attribute is the AudioListener interface object, and it has the following attributes:

position/position/positionZ - They are all AudioParam interface types, which define the position coordinates of the listener. The default value is (0,0,0), which is at the origin of the coordinate system.

forward/forwardY/forwardZ – Their type is AudioParam, which define the vector that the listener faces, that is, from (0,0,0) to (forwardX, forwardY, forwardZ), and the default value is (0, 0, -1), which is the opposite direction of the Z axis.

upX、 upY、 upZ – Their type is AudioParam, which defines the head orientation of the listener, that is, from (0,0,0) to (upX, upY, upZ), and the default value is (0,1,0), which is the Y-axis direction.

Here is an example to achieve the effect shown in Figure 4.26.

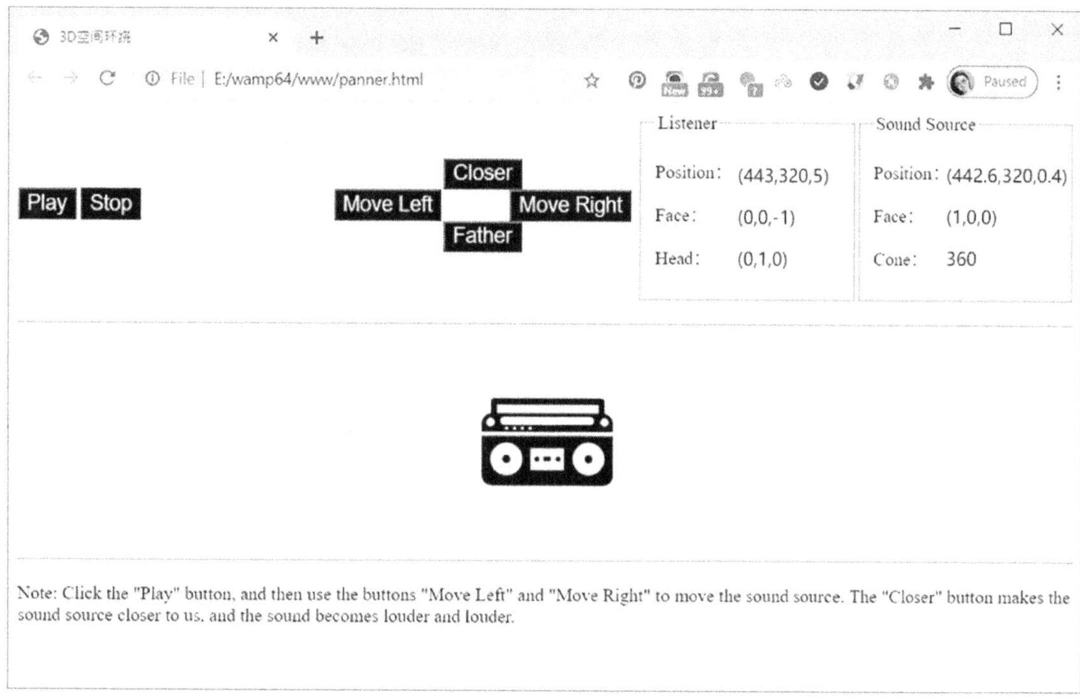

Figure 4.26 Example of 3D surround node usage

The webpage code refers to the following three files, panner.html, panner.css and panner.js. If you have a 5.1 sound system, I suggest you change the Y and Z axis coordinates to experience the real 3D surround effect.

The content of the panner.html file is as follows:

```html
<!DOCTYPE html>
<html>

<head>
    <meta charset="UTF-8">
    <meta name="viewport" content="width=device-width, initial-scale=1.0">
    <title>3D Space Surround</title>
    <link rel="stylesheet" href="panner.css">
</head>

<body>
    <section id="menu">
        <div>
            <button id="play">Play</button>
            <button id="stop">Stop</button>
        </div>
        <div>
```

```html
            <p><button id="come">Closer</button></p>
            <p><button id="right">Move Left</button><button id="left">Move Right</button></p>
            <p><button id="away">Farther</button></p>
        </div>
        <fieldset>
            <legend>Listener</legend>
            <p id="listener">Position : </p>
            <p id="face">Face : </p>
            <p id="head">Head : </p>
        </fieldset>
        <fieldset>
            <legend>Sound Source</legend>
            <p id="panner">Position : </p>
            <p id="arrow">Face : </p>
            <p id="degree">Cone : </p>
        </fieldset>
    </section>
    <section id="main">
        <div class="pulse-wrapper">
            <div id="image-box"></div>
        </div>
    </section>
    <p> Note: Click the "Play" button, and then use the buttons "Move Left" and "Move Right" to move the
sound source. The "Closer" button makes the sound source closer to us, and the sound becomes louder and
louder.</p>

</body>
<script defer src="panner.js"></script>

</html>
```

The content of the panner.js file is as follows:

```javascript
let WIDTH = window.innerWidth;
let HEIGHT = window.innerHeight;

let xPos = Math.floor(WIDTH / 2);
let yPos = Math.floor(HEIGHT / 2);
let zPos = 0;

const play = document.getElementById("play");
const stop = document.getElementById("stop");
const pulseWrapper = document.querySelector('.pulse-wrapper');
const listenerData = document.getElementById("listener");
const pannerData = document.getElementById("panner");
const boomBox = document.getElementById("image-box");
const leftBtn = document.getElementById("left");
const rightBtn = document.getElementById("right");
const comeBtn = document.getElementById("come");
const awayBtn = document.getElementById("away");
```

```javascript
const AudioContext = window.AudioContext || window.webkitAudioContext;
let audioCtx;
let panner;
let listener;
let source;

let boomX = 0;
let boomY = 0;
let boomZoom = 0.50;

stop.setAttribute('disabled', 'disabled');
play.addEventListener("click", function() {
    init();
    source.start(0);
    play.setAttribute('disabled', 'disabled');
    stop.removeAttribute('disabled');
    pulseWrapper.classList.add('pulsate');
})

stop.addEventListener("click", function() {
    source.stop(0);
    stop.setAttribute('disabled', 'disabled');
    play.removeAttribute('disabled');
    pulseWrapper.classList.remove('pulsate');
})

function init() {
    audioCtx = new AudioContext();
    panner = audioCtx.createPanner();
    listener = audioCtx.listener;
    panner.panningModel = 'HRTF';

    leftBound = (-xPos) + 50;
    rightBound = xPos - 50;

    xIterator = WIDTH / 150;

    listener.positionX.value = xPos;
    listener.positionY.value = yPos;
    listener.positionZ.value = 5;
    document.getElementById("face").textContent = "Face : (" + listener.forwardX.value + "," +
listener.forwardY.value + "," + listener.forwardZ.value + ")";
    document.getElementById("head").textContent = "Head : (" + listener.upX.value + "," + listener.upY.value +
"," + listener.upZ.value + ")";
    document.getElementById("arrow").textContent = "Face : (" + panner.orientationX.value + "," +
panner.orientationY.value + "," + panner.orientationZ.value + ")";
    document.getElementById("degree").textContent = "Cone : " + panner.coneInnerAngle;

    listenerData.innerHTML = 'Position : (' + xPos + ',' + yPos + ',5)';

    function positionPanner() {
```

```javascript
        panner.positionX.value = xPos;
        panner.positionY.value = yPos;
        panner.positionZ.value = zPos;
        pannerData.innerHTML = 'Position : (' + xPos.toFixed(1) + ',' + yPos + ',' + zPos.toFixed(1) + ')';
    }

    function getData() {
        source = audioCtx.createBufferSource();
        request = new XMLHttpRequest();

        request.open('GET', 'beijingbeijing.mp3', true);
        request.responseType = 'arraybuffer';
        request.onload = function() {
            let audioData = request.response;

            audioCtx.decodeAudioData(audioData, function(buffer) {
                    myBuffer = buffer;
                    source.buffer = myBuffer;

                    source.connect(panner);
                    panner.connect(audioCtx.destination);
                    positionPanner();
                    source.loop = true;
                },
                function(e) {
                    console.log("Failed to get audio source:" + e.err);
                });
        };
        request.send();
    }

getData();

    function moveRight() {
        boomX += -xIterator;
        xPos += -0.066;

        if (boomX <= leftBound) {
            boomX = leftBound;
            xPos = (WIDTH / 2) - 5;
        }

        boomBox.style.webkitTransform = "translate(" + boomX + "px , " + boomY + "px) scale(" +
boomZoom + ")";
        boomBox.style.transform = "translate(" + boomX + "px , " + boomY + "px) scale(" + boomZoom + ")";
        positionPanner();
        rightLoop = requestAnimationFrame(moveRight);
        return rightLoop;
    }

    function moveLeft() {
```

```javascript
        boomX += xIterator;
        xPos += 0.066;

        if (boomX > rightBound) {
            boomX = rightBound;
            xPos = (WIDTH / 2) + 5;
        }

        positionPanner();
        boomBox.style.webkitTransform = "translate(" + boomX + "px , " + boomY + "px) scale(" +
boomZoom + ")";
        boomBox.style.transform = "translate(" + boomX + "px , " + boomY + "px) scale(" + boomZoom + ")";
        leftLoop = requestAnimationFrame(moveLeft);
        return leftLoop;
    }

    function zoomIn() {
        boomZoom += 0.05;
        zPos += 0.066;

        if (boomZoom > 4) {
            boomZoom = 4;
            zPos = 4.9;
        }

        positionPanner();
        boomBox.style.transform = "translate(" + boomX + "px , " + boomY + "px) scale(" + boomZoom + ")";
        zoomInLoop = requestAnimationFrame(zoomIn);
        return zoomInLoop;
    }

    function zoomOut() {
        boomZoom += -0.05;
        zPos += -0.066;

        if (boomZoom <= 0.5) {
            boomZoom = 0.5;
            zPos = 0;
        }

        positionPanner();
        boomBox.style.transform = "translate(" + boomX + "px , " + boomY + "px) scale(" + boomZoom + ")";
        zoomOutLoop = requestAnimationFrame(zoomOut);
        return zoomOutLoop;
    }

    leftBtn.onmousedown = moveLeft;
    leftBtn.onmouseup = function() {
        window.cancelAnimationFrame(leftLoop);
    };

    rightBtn.onmousedown = moveRight;
```

```javascript
        rightBtn.onmouseup = function() {
            window.cancelAnimationFrame(rightLoop);
        };

        comeBtn.onmousedown = zoomIn;
        comeBtn.onmouseup = function() {
            window.cancelAnimationFrame(zoomInLoop);
        };

        awayBtn.onmousedown = zoomOut;
        awayBtn.onmouseup = function() {
            window.cancelAnimationFrame(zoomOutLoop);
        };
}
```

The content of the panner.css file is as follows:

```css
#menu {
    display: flex;
    justify-content: space-between;
    align-items: center;
}

#menu div {
    display: inline-block;
    width: 200px;
    height: 100%;
}

fieldset {
    width: 180px;
    display: inline-block;
    border: 1px solid grey;
}

button {
    font-size: 18px;
    color: white;
    background-color: black;
}

#come {
    width: 70px;
}

#away {
    width: 70px;
}

div p {
```

```css
    margin: 0px;
    text-align: center;
}

#right {
    margin-right: 60px;
}

#main {
    height: 40vh;
    margin: 20px 0px;
    border-top: 1px solid grey;
    border-bottom: 1px solid grey;
    position: relative;
    justify-content: center;
    display: flex;
    align-items: center;
    overflow: hidden;
}

#image-box {
    width: 231px;
    height: 150px;
    background: url(radio.fw.png) no-repeat;
    background-size: 100% 100%;
    -webkit-transform: scale(0.5);
    transform: scale(0.5);
    z-index: -100;
}

.pulse-wrapper {
    -webkit-transform-origin: center;
    transform-origin: center;
}

.pulsate {
    -webkit-animation: pulse 0.5s linear infinite alternate;
    animation: pulse 0.5s linear infinite alternate;
}

@-webkit-keyframes pulse {
    from {
        -webkit-transform: scaleY(1);
    }
    to {
        -webkit-transform: scaleY(1.07);
    }
}

@keyframes pulse {
    from {
        transform: scaleY(1);
```

```
}
to {
    transform: scaleY(1.07);
}
}
```

4.11 Distortion

The WaveShaperNode node can be used to perform nonlinear distortion on the audio amplitude (volume). Set the distortion function to y=f(x), that is, for a sampling point of input data x, the output is y, as long as f is a non-linear function, then can realize non-linear distortion sound. The input sampling point data generally fall in the [-1,1] interval, and the computer cannot represent a continuous function, but can only use several coordinates on the function curve to approximate the analog function, as shown in Figure 4.27.

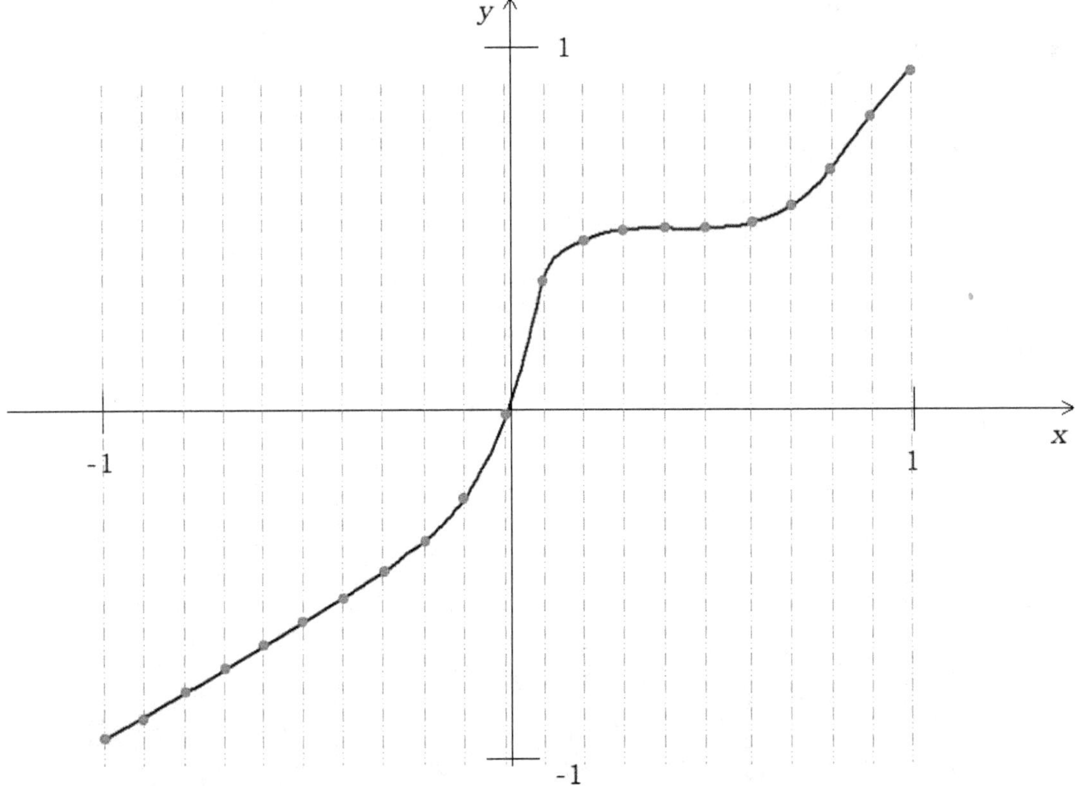

Figure 4.27 Multi-point linear interpolation simulation function curve

For example, the step on the abscissa axis is s, then it s ok just to record the ordinate f(-1), f(-1+s), f(-1+2s), f(-1+3s),..., f (1). When restoring the function in the computer, use a straight line to fill in between two adjacent points, that is, the coordinates of the two adjacent points (-1+n*s, f(-1+n*s)), (-1+(n+1)*s, f(-1+(n+1)*s)). Obviously the smaller the step s, the more ordinates will be recorded, so the restored function is closer to the original function curve.

Use AudioContext.createWaveShaper() to instantiate a sound distortion processing node WaveShaperNode, which has two properties:

curve – It is an array of Float32Array type, which stores several ordinate values of the distortion function. Assuming that the number of array elements is N, then the step of abscissa $s = \frac{1-(-1)}{N-1} = \frac{2}{N-1}$. For input x, the calculation formula of output y is:

$$y = \begin{cases} C[0] & ,v < 0 \\ C[N-1] & ,v \geq N-1 \\ (1-f) \times C[k] + f \times C[k+1] & ,other \end{cases}$$

$$v = \frac{x+1}{2} = \frac{(N-1)}{2}(x+1)$$

where $\frac{x+1}{2}\Big/(N-1)$, $k = \lfloor v \rfloor$, C stands for curve array, $f = v - k$. Since the value range of x is [-1,1], the value range of x+1 is [0,2], and k is the array subscript mapped by the input x. In actual programming, generally n points are equally divided in the interval $x \in [-1,1]$ according to a specific continuous function.

oversample – This property of the WaveShaperNode interface is an enumerated value indicating if oversampling must be used. Oversampling is a technique for creating more samples (up-sampling) before applying a distortion effect to the audio signal. Once applied, the number of samples is reduced to its initial numbers. This leads to better results by avoiding some aliasing, but comes at the expense of a lower precision shaping curve. The possible oversample values are: 'none'(Do not perform any oversampling), '2x'(Double the amount of samples before applying the shaping curve), '4x'(Multiply by 4 the amount of samples before applying the shaping curve).

Here is a practical example, the audio processing directed graph is shown in Figure 4.28.

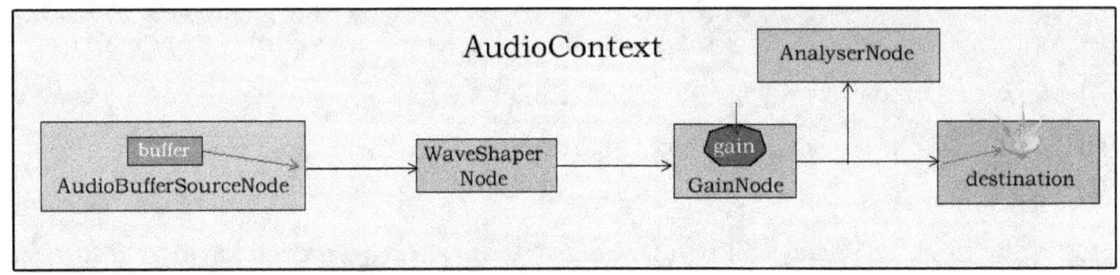

Figure 4.28 Directed graph of sound distortion processing

The reference code is as follows:

```html
<!DOCTYPE html>
<html>

<head>
    <meta charset="UTF-8">
    <meta name="viewport" content="width=device-width, initial-scale=1.0">
    <title>AutoContext: Non-linear Distortion</title>
</head>

<body>
    <canvas id="visualizer" height="120px" width="800px"></canvas><br>
    <input type="file" name="music" id="filePicker" accept="audio/*">
    <input id="volume" type="range" min="0" max="100" value="50"><span>Volume</span>

    <script>
        var canvas;
        const audioCtx = new(window.AudioContext || window.webkitAudioContext)();
        const bufferSource = audioCtx.createBufferSource();
        const gain = audioCtx.createGain();
        const distortion = audioCtx.createWaveShaper();
        const analyser = audioCtx.createAnalyser();

        bufferSource.connect(distortion).connect(gain).connect(audioCtx.destination);
        gain.connect(analyser);
        distortion.curve = generateWaveShapingCurve(65536);
        distortion.oversample = '4x';

        function playMusic(evt) {
            const musicBuffer = evt.target.result;
            audioCtx.decodeAudioData(musicBuffer).then((decodeAudio) => {
                bufferSource.buffer = decodeAudio;
                bufferSource.loop = true;
                bufferSource.start();
                visualize();
            }).catch((error) => console.log(error));
        }
```

```javascript
function readFile(evt) {
    var reader = new FileReader();
    reader.addEventListener("load", playMusic);
    reader.readAsArrayBuffer(evt.target.files[0]);
}


function generateWaveShapingCurve(amount) {
    var curve = new Float32Array(amount);
    let s = 2 / (amount - 1);


    for (let i = 0; i < amount; ++i) {
        let x = i * s - 1;
        curve[i] = Math.atan(5 * x) / (0.5 * Math.PI);
    }
    return curve;
}


function gainVolume(evt) {
    gain.gain.value = parseFloat(evt.target.value / 100.0);
}


window.addEventListener("load", () => {
    document.getElementById("filePicker").addEventListener("change", readFile);
    document.getElementById("volume").addEventListener("change", gainVolume);
    canvas = document.getElementById("visualizer");
});


function visualize() {
    const canvasCtx = canvas.getContext("2d");
    analyser.fftsize = 2048;
    const bufferLength = analyser.frequencyBinCount;
    const dataArray = new Uint8Array(bufferLength);

    var linear = canvasCtx.createLinearGradient(0,0,0,canvas.height);
    linear.addColorStop(0, "red");
    linear.addColorStop(0.7, "blue");
    linear.addColorStop(1, "green");

    draw()

    function draw() {
        const hWIDTH = canvas.width / 2;
        const HEIGHT = canvas.height;

        analyser.getByteFrequencyData(dataArray);
        canvasCtx.fillStyle = 'rgb(200, 200, 200)';
        canvasCtx.lineWidth = 2;
        canvasCtx.strokeStyle = linear;
        canvasCtx.fillRect(0, 0, canvas.width, HEIGHT);

        canvasCtx.beginPath();
```

```
            let step = Math.floor(bufferLength * 3.0 / hWIDTH);
            let x = 0;

            for (let i = 0; i < bufferLength; i = i + step) {
                let y = dataArray[i] * HEIGHT / 256;
                canvasCtx.moveTo(hWIDTH + x, HEIGHT);
                canvasCtx.lineTo(hWIDTH + x, HEIGHT - y);
                canvasCtx.moveTo(hWIDTH - x, HEIGHT);
                canvasCtx.lineTo(hWIDTH - x, HEIGHT - y);
                x += 3;
            }
            canvasCtx.stroke();
            requestAnimationFrame(draw);

            }

        }
    </script>

</body>

</html>
```

The browsing effect is shown in Figure 4.29.

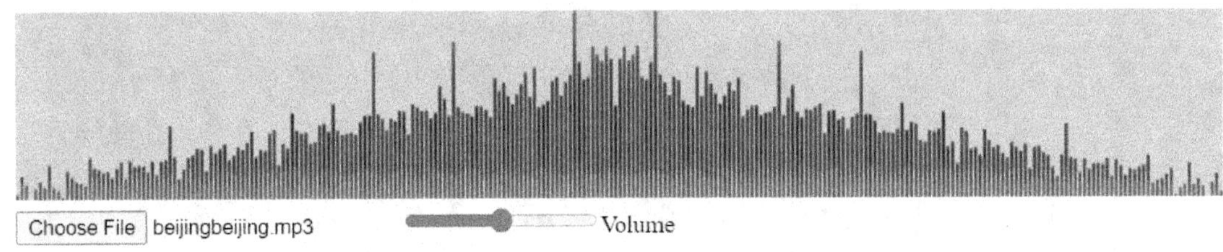

Figure 4.29 Example of Sound Distortion Node

In this example, we use the arctangent function atan(x) as the distortion function. This function increases monotonically in the interval $(-\infty, +\infty)$, and the value of the function falls within $(-\pi/2, \pi/2)$. The variable x in the function generateWaveShapingCurve(amount) is [-1,1], so the value range of 5x is [-5,5]. The curve of atan(5*x) is shown in Figure 4.30.

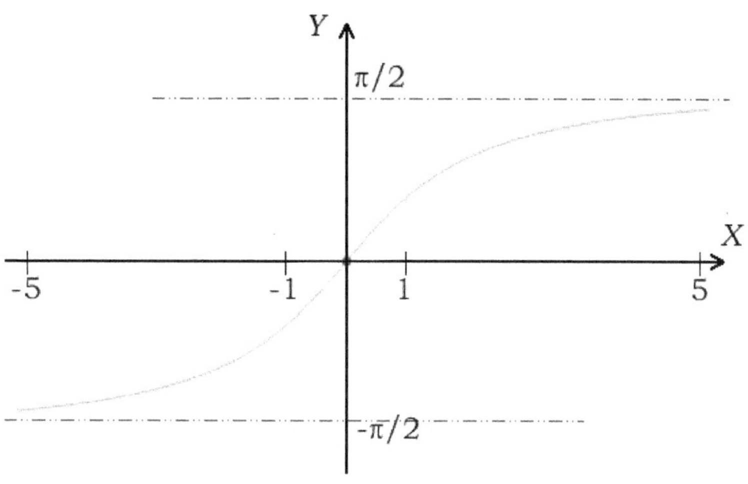

Figure 4.30 atan(5*x)'s curve